A Study Companion to
An Outline of Esoteric Science

A Study Companion to
An Outline of Esoteric Science

Clopper Almon

✐ Anthroposophic Press

Published by Anthroposophic Press

ISBN 0-88010-453-8

Printed in the United States of America

Contents

Foreword **7**

1. The Character of Esoteric Science **19**

2. The Makeup of the Human Being **26**

3. Sleep and Death **38**

4. Cosmic Evolution and the Human Being **49**

5. Knowledge of Higher Worlds: Initiation **106**

*6. Cosmic and Human Evolution:
   Now and in the Future* **121**

Foreword

WE AND THE WORLD AROUND US EVOLVE. This evolution is nowhere more marked than in our own consciousness. When we try to enter into the religious texts of the ancient Egyptians, we have to admit that they are total enigmas to us. Our science would almost certainly be equally incomprehensible to them. They were, for example, obvious masters of what today we call *force* in physics, but they used it completely intuitively, without any *concept* of it. They may well have had visions of force, but no concept. Concepts appear first with the Greeks, and even then they seem to reach only into things of the intellect, logic, geometry, philosophy. Only with the scientific revolution did we grasp with concepts the physical world around us. A new power seemed to unfold in us. Suddenly we could understand that the same force that makes the apple fall holds the moon in orbit. The excitement of the discovery of that new inner capacity swept all before it. What could be understood with this new capacity was Science with a capital *S*; what could not was faith, religion, or superstition according to one's point of view.

Initially, Science was physics and astronomy. Gradually, new domains were conquered; chemistry, geology, biology, economics, and psychology led to a whole new way of looking at the world. Darwin's theory of evolution opened even the question of human origins to the march of Science. One field remained outside the scope of Science, namely, the inner, non-material, spiritual being within each human individual and all the spiritual beings which do not incarnate in human bodies. Religion and myth had long spoken of such beings, but to most students of Science they were invisible, hidden. Some enthusiasts of Science felt that if they themselves did not perceive such beings, then they simply did not exist. Talk of them in myths was merely human behavior to be explained on the basis of material processes. Other, wiser heads recognized that the fact that they did not personally perceive something did not prove that it did not exist, but it did mean that they themselves were in no position to develop a science concerning it. Thus, they lived in a divided world, one of Science and one of Religion.

Rudolf Steiner undertook the enormous work of extending Science into this ultimate domain. Son of a railway station master, he had studied the natural sciences in high school and at what is now called the Technological University of Vienna, then as now the leading technological institute in Austria. He was at home in the natural sciences with their logical, conceptual structure. He admired their care and objectivity. But for him, they left out the essential. For to him, the spiritual beings of which myth and religion spoke were *not* imperceptible but present realities. From a natural gift of "second sight," he had developed a remarkable, controlled clairvoyance which he used as an instrument of scientific investigation. Clairvoyants there had been before. What set Steiner apart was his *conceptual* presentation of the clairvoyantly perceived facts which made them accessible to the understanding of people who cannot themselves directly perceive these beings. As one studies his work, the gap between Science and Religion fades. The inner capacity by which we comprehend the material world begins to comprehend the world of spirit. Our divided world begins to knit together.

There remains, of course, the problem of the perception of the spiritual beings. Can we take an interest in a science of things we cannot perceive? Now in the first place, most modern research in the natural sciences rests on observations which I am in no position to verify for myself. I have to take the word of the scientist reporting his work. I have to trust that if I had spent the many years that he or she spent in preparation and had built similar instruments, then I might also have been capable of having similar experiences. Mostly, however, the natural scientist asks that we follow along in thought. Steiner makes very similar demands. He mainly asks that we follow him in thought and ask ourselves if the thoughts make sense. He is also at pains to explain a path of development leading slowly but safely to the ability to perceive things spiritual for oneself. The difference from the natural sciences is only that the instruments that we must build are our own organs of perception. The process is longer, stretching, most probably, over a number of lifetimes. The first step on that path, however, is the diligent, open-minded study of the results of spiritual research expressed in conceptual form. And that brings us directly to the book with which this study companion is concerned.

This book, *An Outline of Esoteric Science*, also translated as *Occult Science, an Outline,* is Steiner's most complete and methodical presentation of the results of his own spiritual research. Written in 1909, when he was forty-eight years old, it represents his mature thinking, yet also has the careful structure and development characteristic of the work of young authors. The title, *Die Geheimwissenschaft in Umriss* in the original, points out that the subject of the book is just those realities and beings which are, at least initially, hidden from most of us. But at the same time, it makes explicit that this is no collection of "tales of the supernatural" but a clear, conceptual, thoroughly scientific account of these matters. Because the terrain is unfamiliar, a substantial portion of the book must be what might be called "conceptual description." The word *Outline* in the title must also be taken seriously. Nearly every subject discussed here is treated in greater detail in Steiner's other books or lectures. The book is terse, concise, and demands the reader's utmost attention, as well as the energy to visualize inwardly the pictures presented. It is not a book to be skimmed. Nor is it to be sampled here and there — though one man who tried to do so hit a passage that changed his life.

There is no proper English translation for the *Geheim* of the German title. The *heim* is cognate with our "home" and so connotes something intimate, held close, hidden, inner. Hence the "esoteric" in the title of the newest translation, for "esoteric" means fundamentally "inner." Earlier translations used the title *Occult Science.* In Latin, *occult* simply means hence "hidden," but in English *occult* has a fallen meaning which *Geheim* does not have. The book is about the majestic, full spiritual being present in each of us and about the lofty beings above us. *Occult* is clearly not appropriate, but "esoteric" is not much better because it has both a fallen sense and a sense of not being very relevant. My choice would have been *Spiritual Science: An Outline,* for that is the term commonly used by Steiner to describe his work; other good choices might be *The Science of Inner Realities* or, to use Goethe's expression developed in the early pages of the book, *The Science of Manifest Secrets.*

This book is probably not the best introduction to Steiner's work. I would suggest starting with *How to Know Higher Worlds* for a "hands-on," practical introduction to Steiner's approach to self-development. More conceptual but still introductory is *Theosophy,* which is concerned with the structure of the human individual as a being of body, soul, and spirit. It also deals with reincarnation and karma. After one or both of these, *Cosmic Memory* may be appropriate; it describes the evolution

of the earth and of humanity through metamorphosis and reincarnation. At that point, one might want to read some of the lecture cycles available to us only as stenographic transcripts. I
would suggest starting with those given before 1910. Reading
a few of these will soon awaken a desire to see all the ideas put
together and laid out in an orderly fashion. One is then ready
for *An Outline of Esoteric Science.*

Chapter 1 carefully states the nature of this science. Chapter
2 deals with our own inner nature as beings of body, soul, and
spirit. It will recall parts of *Theosophy* but at a deeper level.
Chapter 3, on sleep, death, and reincarnation likewise extends
the ideas from the earlier book. Chapter 4 on evolution, however, is the great advance over what Steiner had previously written. Just as we cannot understand ourselves or any human
without recognizing the reality of reincarnation, so it is also with
the whole world, with the earth itself. To enable us to understand
what stands before us in outer nature as well as our inner nature,
Steiner must take us back through three prior incarnations of the
whole earth and universe. Evolution is the great theme of this
book and, indeed, of Steiner's life work. But it is an evolution
which goes far beyond anything dreamt of in biology or geology
today. Chapter 5 then explains the path of individual spiritual
development. Here one senses an advance over the previous
expositions in *How to Know Higher Worlds* and *Theosophy,* an
advance largely the result, I suspect, of several years of work
with individual students. Chapter 6 looks into the future evolution of the earth. Chapter 7 is really a series of appendices on
various details, not the culmination of the book.

Why should one bother with all this science of the unseen? If
the "seen" makes perfect sense to you as you see it, then this
book is not for you. But if life is full of unanswered questions—
Where did we come from? How can we grow inwardly? Why

is there suffering? Why joy? Why birth? Why death?—then this book was meant for you, as it was meant for me.

If it is indeed a book meant for you, then you are likely to read it several times. For the first reading, if you want to get quickly to the heart of the matter, you can safely skip the prefaces (most of which have been moved to the back of the newest translation) and go straight for chapter 1 and read through to chapter 7. Some readers find this material spellbinding but are full of questions raised by the material. Others find the material challenging, to say the least, and want all the help they can get in holding all the material in mind, making sense of it, and applying it to their own life.

This study companion has something for both types of readers, but *it absolutely assumes that one has read the book—or at least the relevant chapter—before turning to the* Companion. It is organized by chapters in the book; for each chapter there are four elements in the *Companion*:

1. *Themes:* These are brief summaries of the main points of the text. After reading a chapter, you may find it useful to look at the summaries and try to call to mind the details of the exposition back of each summary point. Then close the *Companion* and try to recall the summary as well. When you can do both, you've got the material. This book does not lend itself well to alphabetical indexing. Instead, these summaries should prove useful when looking back to find something in the book after having read it. (There are no summaries of chapter 7; rather these details are mentioned in the Observations section where they are relevant.)

2. *Review Questions:* These are questions to help you to bring before your mind what was said in the chapters. Answers are found in the text of the book.

3. *Discussion Questions:* The answers to these questions are *not* in the text. Some of them are intended to stimulate your thinking about how the material in the book helps you to understand your own experiences. Sometimes they open a discussion of difficult points. You may find them useful either for a discussion group or to start your own thinking on these subjects.

4. *Observations:* These are my own commentary on the text. Some of them try to help with difficult points. Some relate the text to contemporary thinking. Others provide guides for further reading in Steiner's other works or supplement the text with details from these other works. Most of these begin with the (original) paragraph number to which they refer. Those without a number refer to a larger section of text.

The questions and observations have grown out of several study groups and courses devoted to this book. Use them if you find they help. You may prefer the more active course of working out your own study companion—as I did. You may try giving lectures on this material, explaining it carefully to a seemingly empty room. You may, of course, combine the approaches. But it is certain that the more active your involvement with the material, the more helpful Steiner's work will be to you.

Translations

There have been three English translations of this work. The first was *Occult Science: An Outline* by Maud and Henry Monges, published in 1939 by the Anthroposophic Press, then in New York, NY and now in Hudson, NY. In 1962, the Rudolf Steiner Press in London published a new translation by George and Mary Adams; it used the same title as the Monges translation. In 1997, the Anthroposophic Press published a translation by Catherine Creeger with the title *An Outline of Esoteric Science.*

Each translation has its distinctive merits. The Monges translation, for example, often follows the grammar of the German rather closely. This practice makes it great for one who is trying to work through the original with only a modicum of German. At the same time, it makes for rather complicated English. The *Study Companion* was originally written to be printed in the Creeger translation, so the quotations are largely from that translation. That fact should not be interpreted to mean that I generally prefer that translation. If I wish to read this book aloud in English, I go straight for the Adams rendition. Occasionally, the "Observations" will point out significant differences in the translations.

Mechanics

A few mechanical points must be mentioned. The numbers refer to paragraphs in the German text. Since German style of Steiner's time used much longer paragraphs than does contemporary English style, all translators have broken up many of the paragraphs—but in different ways. The only possibility for a standard numbering that can be used with various translations and with the original is to use the numbering of the German paragraphs. These numbers are given in square brackets, e.g. [5], in the Creeger translation. They are not given in either the original German or in the other translations. If you are working with the original, you can, however, easily number the paragraphs. For the other translations, they can be deduced approximately from the "Themes" section. In the original, there are no subheadings; however, in chapters 4 and 5 there are sections separated by an * in the center of a line. In the *Study Companion* I have provided headings for these sections in the Themes section for these chapters. In other chapters, centered headings are totally my own invention.

The GA numbers following the titles of Steiner's works refer to the volume numbers in the official complete edition, *Gesamtausgabe*, of the original German text.

I have given the German chapter titles for clarity of reference.

In transliterations from Greek, I have used é for eta and ó for omega.

The Noblest Word

It has become common in many publications to avoid the use of the word "Man" or "mankind" (except for males) on the grounds that some women feel that they do not include them or that their use somehow shows insensitivity to women's issues, so "human" or "person" are substituted. In the original language of this book, the words *Mensch* and *Menschheit* are absolutely central. How they are translated is not an inconsequential matter, so let us look at the possibilities.

Basically we have *Man* and *mankind* on one side and *human* or *person* on the other. Now the first two come to us from the Germanic or Anglo-Saxon side of our linguistic heritage while the second two come from the Roman or Latin side. Steiner, writing in German, had no choice but to use *Mensch* (which certainly includes women); and a translator into French, Italian, or Spanish would have no choice but to translate it as *homme*, *uomo*, or *hombre*, respectively. But in English, we have a choice. The words have very different histories and connotations.

Of "human," we may read in John Ayto's *Dictionary of Word Origins* (Arcade, NY, NY, 1990):

> *Human* comes via Old French *humain* from Latin *humanus*. Like *homo*, "person," this was related to Latin *humus*, "earth," and was used originally for "people" in the sense "earthly beings" (in contrast with the immortal gods).

Other English words from *humus* include *humble, humility,* and *exhume* (from Latin *humo*, bury).

"Human" points to our connection with the soil, the solid state of the earth. The Hebrew equivalent is Adam, the one who descended into a body composed of solid material. Since *human* is opposed to *divine*, it is used correctly in expressions such as "to err is human; to forgive, divine" or "human frailty." "Humanism" and "humanitarian" both originally referred to the doctrine that the Christ was merely human, without a divine component. We can certainly take a certain pride in our connection with the soil and our mastery of the solid element. But we must be aware that when we use "human" we are emphasizing our *hum*blest member, not the divine spark buried, indeed, "humed" within it.

"Person" is from *persona,* a mask worn by actors in Greek and Roman drama. The mask had a small megaphone built in so that the actor could sound through (*personare*) the mask. "Person" is correctly used where only the outer role, not the inner being matters. It can apply equally to legal persons such as corporations or to natural persons. Our personality is the mask behind which we hide our real selves.

"Man" is the pure expression of the m..n sound. This sound appears where there is a reference to our enduring, thinking spiritual element. Thus it appears in English "mind," in German *Mensch,* in Latin *mens* (mind) and *manere* (to re*main*, be perma*n*ent), in Greek *mneia* memory, in Hebrew *amen* as in "I am the amen." The Egyptians denoted the sound by a picture of a game board to point to thinking and used this sign in the word mn (be firm, to remain) as well as in names such as *Menes* (the founder of Egyptian culture), *Memphis* (his city), or *Amun* (the great god of Thebes). The ancient Hindus called the initiate founder of their civilization *Manu,* which was also their word for Man.

Owen Barfield concluded that "The etymology of the word *man* ... hints at a dim consciousness among the Aryans that the essential function of the human being—at any rate of the Aryan human being—is to think" (*History in English Words*, Lindisfarne Press, Great Barrington, MA, 1985, p. 98). If we want to point to ourselves as thinking beings and especially to what thinks within us, to our spiritual nature, then we use the noblest word of our language and call ourselves *Man* and *Mankind*.

There seems to me to be no contest in which word to choose. Only "Man" and "Mankind" can meet our needs. The notion that they do *not* include women is simply misogynist, for it denies that women think. I had intended therefore to make absolutely clear that when I use the word "Man" or "Mankind" in this study companion, it always *includes* women. Sadly, with a logic that makes my head swim, the publisher held that to use the noblest word to *include* women violated its policy of "gender *inclusive* language." At any point where "human" with its earth-bound connotations could possibly be used, I have felt constrained to use it, though I often felt that the discussion was shifted to a lower plane by doing so. At points where the context made that compromise impossible, you will find the Greek word *anthropos* (plural *anthropoi*). That is a code word between you and me. Quotations, including those from the King James Bible and from earlier translations of Steiner, have been allowed to keep their use of "man" in the generic sense.

If you are incarnated in a feminine body and consider yourself a "thinking being," perhaps you should inform the publisher of what you think of its policy of reserving the noblest word for males only.

I had intended to complement this use of *Man* as a common gender noun by the use of "yoman" where a specifically male person is intended and to resolve neatly the vexed question of the third person singular personal pronouns for impersonal nouns—words like "student," "teacher," "one," "someone," "anyone," "somebody," or "anybody"—by simply dropping the initial *t* from the plural forms. The result is quite readable. The publisher ruled out this neat solution, and we are left with the awkward repetition of "he or she" and "his or her."

§

I would like to thank Robert McDermott for suggesting both to me and to the Anthroposophic Press that I write this study companion. To many students and participants in study groups, I am grateful for stimulation and patience. To Christopher Bamford, Jens Jensen and all of the staff of the Press, I am grateful for their care in going over the manuscript and tolerance of my stubbornness on some points. To my wife, Joan Almon, I am indebted not only for a careful reading and stimulating discussion, but for her infinite forbearance as it became clear that I intended to write the thing *at the dining room table.*

Finally, I would be most interested to receive your comments and suggestions for possible future versions of this study companion. I can be reached by email at almon@inforum.umd.edu or through the publisher.

. . . .

CLOPPER ALMON *was a co-founder of the Rudolf Steiner Institute and has taught courses there on this book and other subjects. He is professor of economics at the University of Maryland, where his professional work is in building quantitative models of economics.*

Chapter 1

The Character of Esoteric Science
Charakter der Geheimwissenschaft

Themes

Natural Science as the Preparation for
a Science of Manifest Secrets

1. The title of the book, *Geheimwissenschaft* (literally, secret science), can call forth all manner of opposition ranging from those who deny that there can be any science of a world that is not material to those who do not want science to intrude in a world that they want left to feeling.

2. The real subject of this book is what Goethe called "manifest secrets," that is, phenomena which remain secret when nature is studied only with the outer senses and the intellect tied to them, but which can open themselves to an inner eye. Can they be the subject of a science? What is or is not science is not determined by the subject matter but by the attitude of soul and mode of thought applied. That attitude and mode developed and schooled in the natural sciences is here applied to these "manifest secrets."

3. The real significance of natural science for the human soul is not the knowledge acquired but the rigor of conceptual ability (*Strenge der Vorstellungsart*) gained. Then, through the soul's strength, this rigor can be preserved in thinking about other areas. 4. The sense world has "guard rails" against inaccurate

thinking which are lacking in the non-sensory world. Hence, when people have spoken about the world's non-sensory content without preparation in the ordinary sciences, a lot of non-scientific talk has resulted. But the problem is the lack of preparation, not the task itself.

5. Whether one who aspires to speak of *Geheimwissenschaft* is justified in doing so can only be decided by others who consider his or her work carefully.

6. The nature of proof in spiritual science is different from that in natural sciences, for in spiritual science just grasping the facts carries with it the proof.

7. All spiritual science arises from two thoughts: 8. First, that behind the sense world there is another, at first invisible, hidden world and, second, that it is possible to penetrate this world through the development of capacities that slumber in the human being.

Various objections to these thoughts arise. 9. One denies the existence of this hidden world and affirms that, eventually, all questions can be answered from the sense world. 10. Another says we cannot know whether or not this other world exists, but we can certainly know nothing of it. 11. Another calls it presumptuous to try to extend knowledge to an area that should be the preserve of faith. 12. Yet another argues that personal opinions about the supersensible prevent any scientific certainty. 13. And there are other objections.

Replies to these objections: 14. To the first, visible facts point to this hidden world. We are naturally full of questions to which there is not the slightest prospect of getting an answer from the sense world alone. 15. With the second, the limits of knowledge objection, one must agree as long as one has in mind only knowing that is based on sense perception. But may there not be other ways of knowing? 16. As to presumption, is it presumptuous to know if one *can* know? 17. And as to the fourth, the view that personal opinions prevail everywhere in the supersensible results from approaching the highest truths on personal whim. In fact, all who go far enough come to the same insight in these matters.

Consequences of Undertaking the Study of Spiritual Science

18. Everyone can find the way to the manifest secrets and to the conviction that they can be opened to them. Entering upon this way opens a source of strength and enthusiasm for life; refusing it leads eventually to loss of interest even in outer things. 19. Eventually, through their own weakness, those who refuse to follow a path of spiritual development become impediments to the development of the whole world in which they live. 20. In fact, however, this denial of the other world goes no deeper than the intellect. Feelings and aspirations hold out for some time against the intellectual denial. 21. A way of knowing that makes the hidden manifest is immediately welcomed by these forces so that it leads to new strength and steadfastness in life. 22–23. Indeed, it strengthens the sources from which spring the soul and spiritual part of anthropos.

24. Thoughtful reading of communications from a spiritual researcher continues the researcher's spiritual work and begins to open the way to spiritual development in the reader. Where the author describes, in subsequent chapters, what he believes he knows about birth, death, and the evolution of the world, he is in no way putting forth a dogma but rather providing material for active spiritual experience by the reader, who is thus prepared for the specific exercises of chapter 5. 25. These exercises are the

means by which the spiritual researcher forges the instruments that any scientist must employ. The only difference is that in this case the instrument is the researcher's own self.

Review Questions

What is the subject matter of spiritual science?

What must the scientist of the spirit learn from natural science?

From what two thoughts does spiritual science arise?

What objections does Steiner mention to these thoughts? How does he answer them?

What sort of effects on our ordinary daily life should result from the study of spiritual science? Why?

In the next three chapters, Steiner will present a wealth of information which the reader has, at first, no way of checking. Is this procedure dogmatic?

Discussion Questions

Steiner insists that the study of the sense world forces us to ask questions to which there can evidently be no answer in the sense world, questions which point to "manifest secrets." What are some such questions? What might such "secrets" be?

Great importance is given to the attitude of the soul developed in natural science. How would you characterize that attitude? Why is it essential in spiritual investigation?

How does the view of what constitutes "science" developed here compare to what you may have learned in natural science courses? Which seems to get to the essence of the matter?

Steiner admits that he will impart a lot of information in the next three chapters, information that might be called "theory" in the natural sciences, that is, concepts that have withstood considerable testing by observation. You will probably have no direct way of verifying most of what he says. How similar or different is this procedure from what you experienced in natural science courses? What sort of confirmation do you think you can expect as you read?

Observations

2. The word *science* derives from the Latin word for "know." (German *Wissenschaft* was derived from it by translating the Latin roots into German.) By rights, it should be applicable to any sort of knowing, not arbitrarily limited in subject matter to the "natural" sciences. Unfortunately, it is still all too easy to find statements like the following in the first pages of university texts intended for the first course in various sciences.

The pursuit of scientific knowledge must be guided by the physical and chemical laws that govern the existence and interactions of atoms, subatomic particles, molecules, and so on. Scientific knowledge must explain what is observed by reference to natural law without requiring the intervention of any supernatural being or force. (Cleveland P. Hickman, Jr., et al., *Integrated Principles of Zoology*, 7th ed., Times Mirror, St. Louis, 1984, p. 7)

What "natural" means is not explained, but it pretty clearly relates to the world of "atoms, subatomic particles, molecules" and the like. There is no room in that definition for economics, not to mention sociology, psychology, anthropology, linguistics, or—heaven forbid—a science of manifest secrets.

But clearly *science* is too valuable a word to be so narrowly limited. Steiner's concentration on "attitude of soul," not subject or process, as the key element of science—as opposed to technology or advocacy (which also use observation and reasoning)—is an important insight quite aside from the present context.

6. What Steiner says about the nature of proof in spiritual science is strikingly like proof in mathematics. It is not unusual in a mathematics book to read through a narrative discussion and then find it summarized as a theorem which needs no further proof. Just grasping all the facts constitutes the proof.

21–23. The comments about the life-strengthening effects of the study of spiritual science have been richly borne out in my own experience and observation. To me personally one of the clearest evidences that anthroposophy was not only safe but valid was the interest it awakened in all sorts of matters I would otherwise have found boring. Boredom, in fact, is not a problem which afflicts many students of Steiner's work.

§

To your thoughts about the nature of the "soul attitude" of science I would like to add my own. I feel that it begins with careful, open-minded observation, but then thinking has to come in to order the observations, to decide what is essential and leave aside the unessential, and then try to find some way to summarize the observations in concepts. The attitude of soul is throughout that of listening, of urging the world to speak to us either as we observe externally or search for concepts. Note that with this idea of science there is no difficulty in making the study of law or politics or history a science. Indeed, Steiner's point is that there is no limit on the subject matter of science.

What role do emotion and will play in science? Don't say "none." In the first place, feeling is the guide of the individual scientist in the choice of subject. Don't go into physics if you don't like it. Moreover, deciding what is good science, what is exciting science is very much a matter of feeling. In mathematics, there is a great difference between a messy, complicated proof and a beautiful, elegant one. But the difference is esthetic. A friend of mine once asked an eminent mathematician what a "proof" meant to him. "It's a feeling," was the wise reply coming from a profound study of twentieth century abstract mathematics. Nonetheless, there is a moment in science when all sympathy or antipathy must be silent, when we must open ourselves without assent or dissent to what we behold either in the world outside us or in the thoughts which well up within us. And what role does will play? Again, determination, the drive to overcome all obstacles, is essential to actually accomplishing science, but there also comes a point when the will also must be silent. We must not let ourselves see only what we want to see.

Chapter 2

The Makeup of the Human Being

Wesen der Menschheit

Themes

1. At the very beginning of a study of the nature of anthropos one meets the physical body and, with it, death. 2–4. Death points to the first of the "manifest secrets": What holds the body together and battles against the disintegration inherent in mineral forces while the body is alive? 5. Supersensible perception observes an independent member of the human being waging this battle, a member which will be called the etheric or life body. 6. To progress as it has recently, it was necessary for natural science to lose sight temporarily of this member, but it can now be recognized by those for whom "the time has come." 8. This etheric body is, as it were, the architect of the physical; to each physical organ corresponds an etheric organ. 9. Every living thing—plant, animal, or human—has its own, individual etheric body.

(In the first printing of the Creeger translation, paragraph 9 of the original was missed in the numbering. It is the short paragraph beginning "Having an ether body...." All of the numbers from 9 on in this printing must be incremented by 1 to match the correct numbers used in the *Study Companion*. Presumably, subsequent printings will correct this problem.)

10. Just as the phenomenon of death points to the "manifest secret" of the etheric body, so does that of sleep point to what

will be called the astral body. Supersensible perception sees this member joining the physical and etheric bodies on waking and departing on falling asleep. Each animal also has an individual astral body. Plants do not; they are therefore in a state of perpetual sleep.

11. Just as sleep points to the astral body, so does forgetting point to the fourth member, the I. Without it, we would be conscious only of what is present. But, in fact, we can form wishes and desires which arise from nothing physical in or around us. 12. Individual animals do not have this capacity, for they lack this fourth member. 13. The observation that animals do not have a memory comparable to human memory is in no way based on introspection but on observing the differences in the behavior of humans and animals. A1. (This section is the first of five addenda inserted by the translator into the text.) Perception of the past is what is here called memory; if we chose to use this word for certain phenomena in animals, then we would need another for human memory. 14. Just as sleep refreshes the life forces, forgetting refreshes the astral consciousness and allows us to meet new experiences free and without bias.

15. The dividing line between body and soul lies in the astral element, which we may accordingly subdivide into astral body (or soul body) and sentient soul. A memory called up by an external stimulus is in the astral body; what gives it permanence and enables its recall without external stimulus is the sentient soul. Their union is often called the astral body when precision is not necessary. (Note the threefold structure of the body: physical, etheric, astral.)

16. Within the soul, two further members must be distinguished: the intellectual (or mind or understanding) soul (*Verstandes-oder Gemütsseele*) and the consciousness soul. The mind soul works, through thinking, with what is already in the

soul. In the first instance, this content has come through the work of the sentient soul. The real being of the I, however, has nothing to do with anything external. It points to the third major member of anthropos, the divine spiritual element. The third soul member, the consciousness soul, brings awareness of this spiritual element into the soul. 17. The spiritual element is divine in the sense that it is of the same substance as divine beings, just as a drop of water is of the same substance as the sea without being the sea. 19. Even the consciousness soul can become aware of the spiritual I only by inner activity. The force that makes this I manifest is the same that has created the whole earth.

20. The activity that led to becoming aware of the I must now be directed to the manifest world, in the first instance to the lower members of the soul, which must be purified and transformed. 21. Next this work reaches to the astral body. When transformed by the I, it is called the Spirit Self. 22. Through religion and art the I can work even into the etheric or life body; its transformed spiritual essence is called the Life Spirit. 23. These processes, normally more or less unconscious, can be consciously taken in hand in the process known as initiation. 24. The transformation can be extended even to the physical body; its transformed part is known as Spirit Man.[1] 25. Thus our full being may be seen as having nine members—three

---

1. The Creeger translation follows the practice started in her 1994 translation of *Theosophy* of rendering *Geistesmensch* as "spirit body" instead of the traditional "Spirit Man." The practice is highly confusing because it makes it appear that this member follows in the sequence physical body, etheric body, astral body. It plainly implies that this member is a part of the body, which it is not. The quotations from Steiner given in a footnote on page 54 of that translation of *Theosophy* as a justification of the translation point in exactly the opposite direction: body is transformed into spirit, not Man into body.

related to the body, three to the soul, and three to the spirit. By considering astral body and sentient soul as one element and consciousness soul and Spirit Self as one element, seven members are seen.

Review Questions

Which bodies do we humans have in common with minerals? Plants? Animals?

Return now to the question in chapter 1, What "manifest secrets" can you think of?

What is the ninefold structure of the being of anthropos? the sevenfold?

What is the function of the etheric or life body?

What is the function of the astral body?

Explain why forgetting is to the astral as sleep is to the etheric and death is to the physical?

How can the I work most effectively on the transformation of the astral body? Of the etheric body?

Discussion Questions

Is there any need to assume an etheric or life body? Has it not been shown that proteins can be synthesized from electric discharges though inorganic materials so that life seems to be inherent in the nature of matter?

What is bodily about the etheric or astral body?

What need is there to postulate an astral body? Is it not true that, once we fully understand physiology, we will completely understand, at the level of atoms and subatomic particles, what consciousness is?

Tell all the stories you can about animals who "remembered." Then ask about each, "Was that animal perceiving the past or responding to the present?"

Steiner speaks in this chapter very highly of the value of religion. Why is it so valuable? He himself, however, was not a member of any religious group, in particular, not of the Christian Community for which he wrote, on request, a liturgy. How can one who has the difficulties which he himself must have had in connecting with any organized religion employ religion in working on his or her astral body?

Observations

This chapter parallels closely the chapter by the same name in Steiner's earlier book *Theosophy*. Refer to it for a slightly different and on some points clearer presentation of the same material. It is particularly good on the basic three-way division of body, soul, and spirit.

§

The threefold division of anthropos into body, soul, and spirit follows the ancient Hebrew and Christian tradition. At the end of the first epistle to the Thessalonians, Paul writes, "May the God of peace himself sanctify you wholly; and may your spirit and soul and body be kept sound and blameless at the coming of our Lord Jesus Christ" (5:23). Paul's *pneuma* and *psyche* (spirit and soul) are translating the Hebrew *ruach* and *nefesh* of Paul's native language. *Pneuma*, like *ruach,* basically means "wind, air, breath"; but *ruach* had also been used in the sense of "spirit" since the second verse of Genesis. Paul and the evangelists began to give *pneuma* this extended meaning.

This concept of individualized spirit is rare if not totally absent in earlier Greek philosophy. There was, to be sure, the concept of the *logos*, but Heraclitus pointed out that it was common, shared by all (Fragment 2). More to the point, Aristotle distinguishes five parts of the soul (the nutritive, appetitive, sensory, locomotive, and thinking [*De Anima,* Book 2, Ch. 3]) which correspond roughly to the etheric body, the desire life of the astral, and the feeling, willing, and thinking activities of the soul in Steiner's terms. And "the body plus the soul constitutes the living being," so there is no room for an individualized spiritual element.

The body-soul-spirit trichotomy, however, was fundamental for Origen, the first great Christian theologian. (See, for example, Henri Couzel's *Origen* (Harper and Row, New York, 1989)). Unfortunately, after his time, the teaching slowly faded. Origen himself is reported to have been anathematized by the Fifth Ecumenical Council in 553, though the anathema is not in the official report of the Council. It is certain, however, that Justinian had destroyed all of his writings which his agents could find in the monasteries of the eastern empire. Steiner stated on a number of occasions in 1917 and later that the Eighth Ecumenical Council in 869/70 had anathematized the doctrine of a spiritual member of the human being. That proposition is hard to document; the Council anathematized (in canon eleven) the doctrine of two souls, a notion discussed by Origen in *On First Principles* without taking a position. It is therefore rather clear that "two souls" was not a reference to soul and spirit. Moreover, the Council was declared null and void by the next council some ten years later. Nonetheless, Origen's influence—and with it the teaching of a spiritual element in anthropos—waned during the Middle Ages but was revived somewhat by Pico della Mirandola and Erasmus, who wrote "A single page of

Origen teaches more Christian philosophy than ten of Augustine" (cited by Couzel, p. 267).

In Steiner's work, this ancient truth of the trichotomy reemerges in the central position.

§

The discussion of the etheric or life body will raise many questions about its relation to "mystery" phenomena such as the efficacy of high dilutions in homeopathic medicine, the *Qi* of oriental medicine, Kirlian photography, or the responses of plants attached to lie detectors. Before launching into these questions, however, one should explore Steiner's own expositions further. In the first place, there is the note on the etheric body at the beginning of chapter 7 of this book, as well as numerous other references to the ethers. The origins of the four ethers—life, chemical or sound, light, and heat—and the four physical elements—fire, air, water, earth—in the order of their density are mentioned in chapter 4, paragraphs 65–77. Another description is given in *Cosmic Memory* (a translation of *Aus der Akasha Chronik*, GA 11), chapter ix. For connections with some of the phenomena mentioned above, Steiner's answer to a question after his lecture "The Etherization of the Blood" (October 1, 1911, GA 130) is especially helpful. He says that electricity is light ether fallen to a sub-material condition, while magnetism is the chemical ether fallen still further. In what may have been a reference to atomic energy, he indicated that a "fearful destructive force" derived from fallen life ether would be discovered in the future. Kirlian photography has been advanced as a way of photographing the etheric body. The patterns produced by it are indeed striking. But since it involves both magnetism and electricity, I suspect that it is recording "fallen" ether rather than the living stuff itself. Homeopathy and oriental medicine seem to me closer to working with living ethers.

An interesting presentation of much of this material together with a good, annotated bibliography of works in English up to the time of its appearance may be found in *The Loom of Creation*, Dennis Milner and Edward Smart (Harper and Row, 1976). (The authors are quite sure that they are photographing the ether and cite Rudolf Steiner in support. I am less sure.) More recent material and bibliographic references may be found in *The Secrets of the Soil* by Peter Tompkins and Christopher Bird (Harper and Row, 1989).

§

10. For the reason for the choice of the word *astral* see chapter 3, paragraph 5 and the second section of chapter 7.

11. As an example of the difficulty in translating let me point out the second sentence of this paragraph where Steiner speaks of the I as the member of anthropos *"wodurch er der Krone der zunächst zu ihm gehörigen Schöpfung ist,"* literally "whereby he is the crown of the next to him belonging creation." But the word *zunächst* can mean not only "next" but also "first of all" or "above all" or "to begin with" or "for the moment." What does it mean here? Our translators diverge widely. Monges: "makes him the crown of the creation which belongs to him." Adams: "marks him as the crown of creation—or of that realm of creation to which man belongs." Creeger: "makes us the crown of creation, of the created world that belongs to us at least temporarily." I would probably say "crown of the immediately surrounding creation." In any event, I would not cite this passage as evidence that Steiner expected our imminent demise.

12. The question of animal memory is bound to raise problems. Here are a few thoughts I find helpful.

First ask how much you remember from when you were one or two years old. For most of us, the answer is "nothing"; and if perchance there is something, it is probably very isolated. Now ask how much you remember from when you were six or seven. Probably now your mind floods with pictures that you can still perceive vividly. What is the difference? When you were two, you delighted your parents and grandparents by "remembering" them. You had a vocabulary that amazed them and left any dolphin, gorilla, or other "talking" animal far behind. Why do you now remember nothing of all this glorious age but so much of what happened when you were six? Your I had not yet descended. It was hovering near but not yet *in* your physical, ether, and astral bodies. That "memory" which you then seemed to have was a heightened version of what animals have. It arose when stimulated by an outside object or an inner condition of your body. One might call it a "response" memory because it is always brought forth in consciousness by something external to that consciousness. The "perception of the past" memory which Steiner is talking about might be called, in contrast, the "initiative" memory. It arises within the consciousness from something already inside that consciousness, not through external stimulation.

As a second exercise, ask yourself how often you have been sitting quietly reading or working when, without any external prompting, you suddenly remembered something, jumped up, looked at your watch, and dashed off shouting, "Oh my! I nearly forgot the...." Now ask how often that dog with the great "memory" did something like that. I had a lot of dogs as a boy. They were always up to some mischief and sometimes seemed to have some sense of guilt in the presence of the damage they had done. But they never had any sense, as far as I can recall, of having forgotten or of being late. They responded when there was an outside stimulus; being late or forgetting was totally impossible for them. They could learn tricks, but I never once saw them practicing them if I was not around to give them the stimulus and call the trick "to mind."

The whole capacity of anthropos to progress, to evolve a culture that changes from generation to generation is, paradoxically, due to the power of memory. For it is thinking that makes progress possible, but the raw material of thinking is memory. If we saw animals changing their culture out of inner impulses, if we saw them calling forth inner pictures in one another by talking, then we might reasonably speak of their having memory.

16. The "unspeakable name of God" refers to Exodus 3:13–14: "I am the I am" and to the Jewish practice of never pronouncing the Hebrew name of God but substituting the Greek word *Adonai*, lord.

19. The extraordinary second half of this paragraph parallels very closely what Steiner says in the first lecture of the cycle on the John gospel (Hamburg, May 18, 1908). The force, here introduced as that which makes the divine I manifest to the consciousness soul, he identifies as the *logos* or Word of the first verses of the John gospel: "In the beginning was the Word, and the Word was with God, and the Word was God.... All things were made by him.... And the Word became flesh and dwelt among us." The *logos* creates the world, then the lower elements of the human being and the other living beings and then finally awareness of the I within the consciousness soul. The outward sign of that awareness in us is speech, the Word, which appears nowhere else in creation.

§

The ninefold division of our being is reasonably clear:

BODY:

      Physical
      Ether or life
      Astral

SOUL:

      Sentient
      Mind, understanding, or intellectual
      Consciousness

SPIRIT:

      Spirit Self
      Life Spirit
      Spirit Man

The function of the sentient soul is to bring into our internal awareness the messages from the body. It does this job by coupling strongly with the astral body so that one may speak of the combination as a single unit which I would prefer to call the astral member of our being—rather than the astral *body*. Similarly, the job of the consciousness soul is to bring into the soul's awareness the existence and the messages of the spirit. To do so, it couples strongly with Spirit Self to form another mixed member which Steiner also calls, somewhat confusingly, the Spirit Self. What then always comes as a surprise to me is that the middle element, previously called the Mind soul, gets relabeled as the I, a term previously strongly connected with the spirit. The best explanation that I can offer is that the spirit, the I, which has worked through the instrument of the mind soul to transform the astral, ether, and physical bodies into members of the Spirit, has, in the process, so transformed the Mind soul that it can in its new state be called the I.

The process of transforming body into spirit needs careful thought. If I paint a picture or raise a garden, I am changed by the process. I, my spiritual being, is different long after the picture has been thrown away or the last cabbage eaten. That transformation is what makes these activities fun. It is why being alive is fun. The spirit's involvement with matter changes the spirit just as it changes the matter. That, indeed, is why we, as spiritual beings, incarnate in material bodies. But, you may ask, can matter actually become spirit? In later chapters we will learn that spirit became matter. Is the reverse impossible?

§

A striking application of the sevenfold structure of the being of anthropos is found in the Lord's Prayer. ("The Lord's Prayer, an Esoteric Commentary" a lecture given in Berlin, January 28, 1907, GA 96.) It is a prayer for our whole being, for Steiner associates:

NAME	Spirit self
KINGDOM	Life spirit
WILL	Spirit Man
BREAD	Physical body
DEBTS	Etheric body
TEMPTATION	Astral body
EVIL	I

The Jewish seven-flame candelabra or menorah may be seen as a symbol of the transformation of the three lower members into three higher members, for the lines of the menorah connect the first flame with the seventh, the second with the sixth, and the third with the fifth.

21.09.22

Chapter 3

Sleep and Death

Schlaf und Tod

Themes

1. We explore sleep and death not to flee active waking consciousness but to understand the sources from which it is refreshed. 2. During sleep, the astral separates from the physical and etheric bodies. Supersensible perception is required to investigate what then happens to the astral, but the result of that investigation can be understood by clear thinking and used to understand everyday experience. 3. The astral and I withdraw so that the astral can renew in the astral world the images which it must impart to the etheric body for its shaping of the physical. Sleepiness is a sign that the astral wants to withdraw. 4. The astral body is as dependent on the astral world as the physical body is on the physical world. 5. Hence, the restoration of the astral body by its contact with the astral world makes sleep refreshing. This astral world, incidentally, includes other heavenly bodies besides our earth — hence the name *astral*. 6. Of course, there are physical processes that go with sleep, and they should be studied. But they are to what we are discussing as a finished house is to the plan of the architect. 7–8. Dreaming occurs when the astral has withdrawn from the physical but maintains a certain connection with the etheric. In this state, we see even physical processes around us transformed into symbols.

Dreams of a split I indicate that we have not yet acquired the ability to become aware of it other than through the senses.

9–10. At death, the astral pulls the etheric body with it as it leaves the physical. Astral and etheric remain united for a few days. The forces of the etheric body, formerly used to build up the physical, can now be used to make the processes of the astral body perceptible. 12. While still united with the etheric body, the astral has no new experiences but the etheric enables it to perceive the life just concluded in a series of images spread before it. This perception fades as the etheric body loses a shape corresponding to physical and the astral has to separate from it. Near death experiences sometimes (but not always) involve this memory picture.

13. During life in a body, three types of desires arise: (1) those from the necessities of the body, (2) those coming from the spirit for things spiritual, and (3) those coming from the spirit's pleasure in bodily things in which there is no manifestation of the spirit. The first type falls away immediately after death, and the second type can be satisfied directly in the spiritual world. The third type, such as a longing for good tasting food even when one has no need of nourishment, have to be burned away by the "consuming fire of the spirit." This burning away is necessary for perception in the spiritual world of, for example, a beloved person.

14. During a period of about one third as long as the previous life, the I remains united with the astral body and moves through the experiences of that life in reverse, reversed both in time and in feeling: we feel the pleasure or pain which we brought to others. When this journey is completed, the I separates from the astral; the part of the astral which can live only in consciousness of the outer world becomes a sort of corpse in the astral world. Thus, there are three corpses—physical, etheric, and astral.

15. During the period of purification, desires of the third type (see paragraph 13 above) become food for dark, demonic beings intent upon an evil beyond any in the sense world—the destruction of the human I if it feeds them. After purification, a new consciousness begins for the I; a world streams, as it were, from within.

16. Into this world of the spirit, however, the I brings, in spiritual extract, the fruit of its previous life which now unfolds in and is worked upon by the spirit world. This world manifests in ways resembling light, sound, and words, but the I experiences these as coming from within, not from without. 17. Several realms appear within the spirit world, corresponding in a way to land, water, and air in the physical world. Like the land masses are the spiritual archetypes of things having physical existence; like water, those of life; and like air, those of feelings. In the spirit world, however, objects appear as the complement of their physical counterpart. 18. Similarly, the spiritual origins of thoughts correspond to warmth in the physical world; and the primal beings of wisdom resemble the sun raying forth light. 19. The spirit beings that form our physical body belong to the first of these areas (the one that corresponds to land); those that build the etheric body, to the second; and those that form the astral, to the third.

20. After the period of purification, everything flowing towards the I improves it and gives it new form. When, after a time, the spirit is again ready for incarnation, a new astral body, then a new etheric, and finally a new physical is formed. We are aware of our rebuilding up to the point of the formation of an astral body. Before completion of the etheric, we see a picture of the life to come, of the obstacles which must be overcome to progress in self-development. From this vision arise the forces to deal with these problems. The image of pain inflicted on

another becomes the force to make up for this pain. This connection between an earlier life and a later one is known as the law of destiny or *karma*.

21. Between death and new birth we also work to transform the earth to match the conditions developing within us. 22. We find and work with those to whom we formed a spiritual connection on earth, and this bond can continue into a new physical life. 23. This process repeats itself, but it had a beginning in time and will have an end.

Processes between death and rebirth are, of course, deeply hidden. Yet an awareness of them can throw light on many puzzles that confront us in ordinary life. 24. Why are children born so differently endowed? Some will take the view that everything depends on the external world, on environment, heredity, or chance. But others will recognize that in each child there is an element that is completely new.

25–28. The facts of life between death and rebirth help us to understand life between birth and death. But that, alone, is not sufficient grounds for assuming their truth. There is, however, a stricter test, a test that can be made by anyone quite independently of any direct supersensible perception. The concept that a former life has implanted in us the power to meet a certain event can make that event's inner necessity dawn on us. When we realize that our concept had the force to reveal the facts to us, we recognize its correctness by its fruitfulness. Of course, like any proof, this one is truly convincing only to one who experiences it.

29. Another indication of the truth of these thoughts is found in the experience of education, for every teacher knows that the experiences brought by the teacher are effective only if met by forces coming from deep within the student.

30. Some thinkers, such as I. H. Fichte, reach the point of seeing that there is a spiritual being within each human being but do

not make the step to recognize that this spiritual being has lived before. The problem with this position is that it would imply that each of us, coming straight from the divine source, would be a stranger to what confronts us in life. But that is contrary to experience. Indeed, an unbiased educator can observe: I bring to my student some result from earth experience, something that is quite foreign to all his or her inherited properties and upbringing, and yet it excites him or her as if he or she had had a hand in the work from which that result stems. Thus, our involvement in the past of the earth—in previous earth lives—becomes the only satisfactory explanation for the full range of our experiences.

Review Questions

Why study sleep and death?

Why do we get sleepy?

What happens with our various bodies during sleep?

At what point do dreams arise? What is their particular character?

What happens with the various bodies at death?

What is the source of the memory picture which arises after death? Why and how quickly does it fade?

What are the three types of desires of a spirit dwelling in a body? What happens to each after death?

What is the difference between the way we experience the previous life after death and the way it was experienced during that life?

What domains or realms appear in the spirit world and how do they relate to the physical?

What does the preview of the next life show us?

How can the correctness of these thoughts be proven without spiritual vision?

Discussion Questions

Near death phenomena are now widely known. How do the accounts given, for example, by Raymond Moody in *Life after Life* mesh with Steiner's descriptions given here?

Illustrate the desires of the three types of desires discussed in paragraph 13.

How does the description of the period of burning away of desires of the third type given here fit with the description given in *Theosophy*?

Modern consciousness usually reacts rather strongly against the "hell fire and damnation" doctrines common in an earlier age. Paragraph 15, however, paints a picture as terrifying as anything in Dante's *Inferno*. Or is there a difference?

After purification, most of the time between death and new birth is spent working on the transformation of the earth. What forms might this work take? What sorts of transformations have been wrought by it?

Can you recall incidents in your own life or in that of friends which illustrate the sort of experiences Steiner adduces as "proofs" in paragraphs 23–30?

Observations

3. Fatigue or sleepiness arises because the astral wants to go out of the etheric body for a while so that it can refresh the images which it must impart to the etheric body for its work on the physical body, usually not because the physical is worn out. Steiner illustrates this point (in addendum 3) by the example of someone who, though by no means "worn out," goes to sleep in a dull lecture. This dozing off is just a bit of adaptive behavior

on the part of the astral. Since the physical is caught where it cannot bring the astral anything of interest, the astral wants to use the time to better purpose in the astral world, so the poor wretch is soon yawning and then snoring away in the lecture. Somewhat surprisingly, Steiner speaks of how the soul "becomes absorbed in the enjoyment of its own bodiliness—*im Genuss der eigenen Leiblichkeit aufgeht*—at exactly the moment when the soul is *not* in the body, that is, during sleep. My explanation is that during waking, the soul is absorbed in images of the outer world; during sleep it returns to the images, to the archetypes of the physical body in the spiritual world which it must then in waking life impart to the etheric body to guide its work on the physical. The *Leiblichkeit* is therefore not the material body but its spiritual archetype. Upon waking, the soul finds, not surprisingly, that it needs to rework, reform, put to rights what the physical and etheric bodies have built up during its absence. During sleep, the astral must make itself ready, in Steiner's words, *wieder zurückzubilden* what the physical and etheric built during sleep. Both Creeger and Adams translate this phrase with "undo," which seems too harsh; Monges uses "transform," which seems closer. The idea as I understand it is that, before going to sleep, the etheric body was losing the right image of the physical because the astral was all involved with images of the outer world. Consequently, the work done by the etheric and physical during sleep, important though it is, will not be up to the standards of the astral when it returns with fresh images from the spiritual world. It will have to be reshaped into the right form. Perhaps a short meditation on awakening gives the astral a chance to impart its fresh images to the etheric body before becoming filled with the images from the senses.

7. Students of dreams are likely to find Steiner's discussion here disappointing, for they believe that dreams can tell us

about much more than our physical environment—the covers that are too hot or the picture that fell off the wall. Indeed, I am reminded, as I read these passages, of the fellow who dreamed that he was eating flannel cakes, only to wake up and find the blanket *gone*. Steiner's point, however, is not that all dreams are of this nature but that *even* physical conditions get transformed into extravagant symbols. Any non-physical experience would be subject to as much or more transformation into symbols in a dream. Elsewhere (*How to Know Higher Worlds*) he speaks of the transformation of dream life in the course of spiritual development.

10. The end of this paragraph very briefly makes an important point: in normal sleep, when the astral has withdrawn, the etheric body must work on the physical to restore it. In the earlier exposition, the emphasis was on the need of the astral to withdraw to refresh itself in the astral world. But while present in the etheric and physical bodies, the astral makes demands on the physical for sense impressions or other activities that do indeed wear down the physical. While it is true that this wear is not what makes the astral *want* to withdraw, it is very vital for our health that it *does* withdraw so that the etheric body can restore the organic health of the physical. Nearly everyone notices that wounds and illnesses seem to heal faster when we are asleep. In children, careful observation has shown that most growth occurs during sleep.

13. The third type of desires is most interesting. Steiner's only example is the desire for good tasting food that is unrelated to the need for nourishment. Surely the desire for tobacco, alcohol and certain drugs falls into this category as well. Sexual desires would seem to be particularly tricky here. On the one hand, their satisfaction is necessary to the continuation of life and, like eating of nourishing food when hungry, can certainly

play a role in spiritual development. Yet their abuse is all too easy. They would seem to fit in well with the reference, at the end of the paragraph, to desires for another person which can be satisfied only by means of physical organs. It is most interesting that it is only after these desires have been "burned away" that the beloved becomes visible after death. In the next chapter, we will see that the excess entanglement in matter, brought on by this third type of desire, has radically altered the course of evolution.

14. In his lectures, Steiner frequently refers to the experience of reliving the previous life in reverse as life in Kamaloka, a Sanskrit word meaning "world of desires." In *Theosophy*, Steiner describes this period in terms of the various types of desires which must be burned away. Note carefully that Steiner does not say that the whole of the astral body disintegrates but only the part that "can live only in the consciousness of the outer physical world." The further use of this non-disintegrating part is described in paragraph 20 below.

In lectures from 1909, given at the time that he was working on *An Outline of Esoteric Science,* and gathered into the volume entitled *The Principle of Spiritual Economy* (GA 109), Steiner considerably qualifies the notion that the etheric and astral corpses disintegrate. Those which embody important achievements of their bearers may be reused, woven into the etheric and astral bodies of newly incarnating spirits. Indeed, they may be multiplied and the "copies" reused simultaneously by a number of people at the same time. After numerous specific examples, Steiner states "… most human beings living at present no longer have etheric or astral bodies that were originally woven anew from the general fabric of the world. Almost every human being has in his or her etheric and astral body a fragment that has been preserved from ancient times because the principle of spiritual economy is at work preserving useful elements for repeated utilization" (March 7,1909). It may still be true that most of these etheric and astral corpses decay, for only the best are preserved and copied. Many of the common stories of reincarnation, especially those arising from hypnotism or mediumship, seem to me to relate to the previous experiences of the reused astral or etheric body.

16. The spiritual manifestations analogous to light, sound, and words seem to correspond to the Imaginative, Inspirational, and Intuitive states of consciousness described in chapter V.

17. In projective geometry, a form can be equally well described in terms of points or lines. Thus, a circle can be thought of as all the points equidistant from a given point (the primal definition) or as all the lines equidistant from that point (the dual definition). The similarity to the polarity between physical objects and their spiritual archetypes must account for the importance Steiner placed on projective geometry, for example, in the Waldorf school curriculum.

21–30. Further accounts by Steiner of life between death and rebirth may be found in various lectures. Particularly fine is the six-lecture course *The Inner Nature of Man and Our Life Between Death and a New Birth* (GA 153), given in April 1914 in Vienna. Further information may be found in lectures given in Berlin in 1912–13 and gathered in the volume *Between Death and Rebirth* (GA 142). Many of Steiner's later lectures, especially during World War I, dealt with the connections between the living and the dead, and it is particularly through these connections that the dead work upon the earth. Some of these lectures are gathered in the volumes *Die Verbindung zwischen Lebenden und Toten* (GA 168) and *Das Geheimnis des Todes* (GA 159–160). On a more personal note, the volume *Unsere Toten* (GA 261) contains memorial talks by Steiner for

more than fifty deceased friends. It also contains some twenty
prayers and meditations for spiritual work with the dead. Here
is one of these, which incorporates much of this chapter in a
moving meditation:

>Let our love now follow thee,
>Soul, who lives in spirit world,
>Look upon thy earthly life,
>See and know thyself as spirit.
>May the Self thy spirit finds,
>As it thinks in land of soul,
>Take our love into thee there,
>So we can feel ourselves in thee
>And in our souls thou mayest find
>All that lives in truth with thee.

§

>*Unsre Liebe folge Dir,*
>*Seele, die da lebt im Geist,*
>*Die ihr Erdenleben schaut;*
>*Schauend sich als Geist erkennt.*
>*Und was Dir im Seelenland*
>*Denkend as Dein Selbst erscheint,*
>*Nehme unsre Liebe hin,*
>*Auf dass wir in Dir uns fühlen,*
>*Du in unsrer Seele findest,*
>*Was mit Dir in Treue lebet.*

Chapter 4

Cosmic Evolution and the Human Being
Die Weltentwickelung und der Mensch

Themes

1. The fourfold structure of anthropos is intimately connected with the whole cosmos and its evolution. By studying the evolution of the macrocosm, we will gain deeper insight into the human microcosm. 2. Natural science also recognizes an evolutionary connection between humanity and the earth.

3. Spiritual science, in tracing back the evolution of anthropos, comes to a point at which the I first entered earthly embodiment. 4. At that time, it found the physical, etheric, and astral bodies already developed. 5. To find their origins, we must go further back. 6. As we do so, we first find the material aspect of the earth changing as a manifestation of spiritual forces. Then we reach a point where matter itself condenses out of spirit. 7. A science which only recognizes matter cannot penetrate further back. 8. The spiritual forces that have produced material processes in the past preserve an imperishable record of those events. This *akashic* record can be "researched" by one who has developed the necessary capacities. The accounts of what is thus found, however, can be understood by normal thinking. In fact, following such accounts with clear, active thinking is one of the best preparations for spiritual sight. Such logical thinking can even lead to corrections in the reports of the clairvoyant investigator.

9. Before the purely spiritual state mentioned above, however, can be found a kind of ancient physical planet. Indeed, three earlier incarnations of the earth can be found. 10. It is possible to see primeval events within the events of the present. 11. In the preceding incarnation, there were beings that had the three lower human members but not yet the I. Thanks to the intervening spiritualization, when these beings reappeared on the present earth it eventually became possible for some of them to receive the I. 12. Each of the three earlier incarnations contributed in essential ways to building up the three lower members, so that we must study them to understand ourselves. These earlier incarnations are known as *Saturn, Sun,* and *Moon,* not to be confused with the present bodies by those names. (For clarity, I will italicize these names when they refer to these earlier incarnations of the solar system.) 13–15. Today's words cannot describe precisely these earlier conditions, especially the first two. When we use words such as *light* or *heat* to describe these earlier conditions, the reader will have to bear in mind that they are not exactly the light and heat of today but what this light and heat developed from. (In the paragraph numbers, the first printing of the Creeger translation missed paragraph 14 which begins "This difficulty in finding...." Consequently, all paragraph numbers above 14 in this printing must be incremented by 1 to give the correct original paragraph number.)

Physical, Etheric and Astral Bodies in Evolution

16. The physical body goes back in its origins to *Saturn.* On *Sun* it was reworked so that it could receive the etheric body. On *Moon,* both were further perfected to receive the astral

body, and on *Earth*, all three were transformed to receive the I. Thus, the physical is our oldest, most perfect member and the I is at the beginning of its development. 17. The perfection of the physical compared to the astral is easily seen in the extraordinary perfection of the heart or brain in comparison to the unruly passions of the astral or weakness of the I. Indeed, illnesses of the physical may have their origin in the I and be transmitted to the physical via the astral and etheric bodies, although tracing this effect is complicated by the fact that the cause is in one lifetime while the illness occurs in a subsequent one.

Saturn

18. There was only one "kingdom" physically present on *Saturn*, one corresponding to the present human physical body. Other beings were present but not incarnated below the level of the etheric body. 19. Towards the middle of *Saturn*, this one physical kingdom consisted of beings of warmth. 20. It is difficult for moderns, especially those who have studied physics, to conceive of warmth without something to be warm. But for the spiritual researcher, just as there are the three states of being— solid, liquid, and gaseous—so there is a fourth, warmth. Physics speaks of the effects of this fourth state, but not of its nature.

21. On *Saturn*, the foundations of our present physical bodies were laid in bodies that obeyed physical laws but consisted, near the middle period of *Saturn*, only of warmth. Around them, a series of higher beings worked in seven stages on *Saturn* and were reflected by the bodies. These higher beings, whose lowest element was an astral body, began with (1) Spirits of Will (*Thrones*) who, pouring forth will from their own essence, created the original substance of *Saturn* which was of the nature of will, not yet of warmth. They were followed by

(2) Spirits of Wisdom (*Kyriotetes*), (3) of Motion (D*ynamis*), (4) of Form (E*xousiai*), and (5) of Personality (A*rchai*). Each transformed the *Saturn* beings. The Spirits of Wisdom imparted the ability to reflect life; the Spirits of Motion, the capacity to reflect the feeling of these beings. The Spirits of Form individualized the *Saturn* beings. The Spirits of Personality brought them finally to the state of warmth and to the reflection of their own personalities. 22. The Spirits of Personality reached their human stage in the fifth period of *Saturn*.

23. After their work, a flickering inner life began in the *Saturn* beings. They glow, then shine. Then the (6) Spirits of Fire (A*rchangeloi*) entered, and, through the cooperation of exalted Spirits of Love (S*eraphim*), have sensations through the *Saturn* bodies, though they still had no I consciousness. Their work laid the basis of human sense organs.

24. *Saturn*'s interior became like surging sensations of taste but radiated outward a sort of music. Here entered (7) the Sons of Twilight or Sons of Life (*Angeloi*), the angels. With the aid of the exalted Spirits of Harmony or *Cherubim*, they developed a plant-like consciousness akin to dreamless sleep and began a form of metabolism.

25. By the last stage of *Saturn*, the *Saturn* bodies, with the help of the Spirits of Will, acquired a consciousness comparable to that of minerals today and laid the basis of Spirit Man. Smells were the inner—and a mechanical sort of I, the outer— manifestation of this work.

26. Thus, we find first something like warmth, then light, then taste and sound, then smells and a mechanical I. Before the warmth stage were stages which can be likened only to certain inner soul states. 27. Time itself begins in the fourth stage of *Saturn*. 28. It is pointless to seek origins earlier than *Saturn*. 29. The higher beings, such as the Spirits of Will, worked during

all of *Saturn* but were most prominent in the phases indicated. 30. The higher beings acquired new capacities on *Saturn*. After their activity there they needed to withdraw, as does our astral body and I during sleep, to other worlds to transform these abilities and prepare for new activity. *Saturn* dies away. All the actors we have met on *Saturn* will return on *Sun* but with enhanced abilities. First, *Saturn* must be recapitulated to regain the starting point in the new conditions.

Sun

31. On *Sun*, the human being acquired an etheric body and reached the stage of consciousness now present in plants. After a recapitulation of *Saturn* during the first *Sun* cycle to reestablish the physical body in the new conditions, the Spirits of Wisdom (in the second half of the first *Sun* cycle) poured the etheric body into the physical. 32. During a period of rest (between the first and second cycles of *Sun*), the previously united *Sun* beings split into an etheric and an etheric-penetrated physical component. Then (middle of the second cycle), the Spirits of Motion entered the etheric and gave it the capacity to cause inner movement in the physical. 33. At this time, the air separated from the warmth. Humans became glowing warmth structures with inner air forms moving like sap in plants. After a second rest, Spirits of Form gave permanence to the shapes of these beings.

34. After a third period of rest, we come to *Sun*'s middle (fourth) cycle. Spirits of Love began to make themselves felt in these etheric bodies, and the Spirits of Personality, who had now reached the Imaginative level of consciousness, beheld this activity. This combined activity made the etheric body capable not only of transforming the gaseous physical body but also of reproduction.

35. Not all of the beings produced when the Spirits of Wisdom brought forth the physical bodies at the beginning of *Sun* were capable of receiving an etheric element. Some remained at the *Saturn* state. This *Saturn* warmth substance was divided into two parts. One part was absorbed into the physical body of the *Sun* humans. The Spirits of Fire were then working in this body, and they used this *Saturn* material to develop their consciousness to what we presently have, just as the Spirits of Personality had used this material on *Saturn*. The other part became a second kingdom beside the human kingdom. It had only a physical body. Likewise, there were Spirits of Personality that had remained at their *Saturn* state. They were attracted to this second kingdom. Together, they withdrew to a second cosmic body, a Saturn during the *Sun* incarnation, where they could work together as they had on *Saturn* and ray warmth forces into the main sun body. 36. As the Spirits of Fire worked on the *Saturn* nature in the physical bodies of the "normal" *Sun* beings, they produced precursors of our sense organs, while in the etheric element, the Spirits of Personality and Love produced the origin of our glandular system. They also created a dim perception of the other kingdom.

37. In the second half of the fifth *Sun* cycle, Sons of Life, the angels, cooperate with the Spirits of the Harmonies. And in the second half of the sixth cycle, the human beings themselves begin to work in the etheric in cooperation with the Spirits of Wisdom. By the first half of the seventh period, they have achieved a dreamless sleep consciousness, and the germ of Life Spirit was created. 38. *Sun* now dissolves into a cosmic sleep so that all the beings can metamorphose their accomplishments for rebirth in the next planetary incarnation.

Moon

39. *Moon* began with a recapitulation of *Saturn*, a rest, and then one of *Sun*. In its second half, the Spirits of Motion bestowed the astral element on the human beings; and pleasure and displeasure began for them. After a second rest, Spirits of Form entered and instinctive longing and desire arose in the humans. 40. The physical body acquired a liquid or water component. 41. Two other kingdoms appeared beside the human kingdom, one of beings still at the *Saturn* stage, one of beings at the *Sun* stage. The *Moon* body split into two, one a refined sun where higher beings work and the other, with the human forms, the actual *Moon* incarnation of the earth. On the second, the Spirits of Form continued their work, making all three elements denser.

42. In all evolution, a new being is first separated from the environment and then the environment reflects itself in that being until it can develop further independently. So the *Moon* first reflects back the sun. But then a rebellion arose by beings (identified in paragraph 81 as Luciferic) who seized some of the will substance left from the beginning of *Saturn* and used it to shape a life independent of the sun beings. 43. The sun beings ennobled the gaseous and warmth elements of the humans. 44. The rebels worked upon the watery element, making it more independent. The conflict between the two influences was equilibrated by sun beings making the material element fragile and perishable. When humans shed this material garment, they were dependent solely on the sun beings; when they put it on, the rebel *Moon* beings also worked on them.

45. The mineral-plants, plant-animals, and animal-humans of the *Moon* displayed great variety. 46. This variety reflected the influences of higher spiritual beings who had remained at

earlier stages of development, as well as those that were normally developed. In fact, a whole solar system with a number of planets came into existence.

47. During a third pause, the human astral bodies were worked on particularly strongly by the sun beings. When they reentered the lower members at the beginning of the fourth cycle, they refined these lower members to receive the Spirits of Personality in the astral and the Spirits of Fire in the etheric during the second half of this cycle. 48. Under their influence, processes of breathing and digestion appeared. Forming of mental images in dream-like consciousness closely resembled reproduction. The symbols of this dream consciousness worked strongly on the whole being.

49. After a fourth pause, evolution proceeded with the emergence of a head, which was strongly under the influence of the images of its own consciousness, and of a main body which was directly influenced by the sun beings. 50. The spiritual beings arranged for the moon to rotate around the sun, thereby achieving a rhythmic balance between the sun forces and the independent moon forces. The beings on the moon also moved about, seeking or avoiding the sun forces. 51. The Sons of Life (angels) at this time worked in the physical bodies and reached the stage of consciousness we now have. 52. Two states of consciousness arose, one duller but more united with the cosmos when turned toward the sun, one clearer but more limited when away from it. During the sun time, the astral was freed from the physical and was as if intoxicated with the cosmic harmonies. During the time away from the sun, the main body hardened; as the sun time approached, this old body had to be cast off, shed like last year's skin, and the being rose out of it newly configured. Thus a sort of reproduction and a sort of death and birth appeared, but the same being moved into the new body.

Each human also felt connected to a Son of Life, an angel. 53. What the Son of Life perceived of its reflection in the human astral bodies belonging to it provided it with an I-conscious-ness. The human being's interaction with the Son of Life led to the beginning of the nervous system in the physical body.

54. In the middle period (evening of the fourth cycle), Spirits of Personality implanted independence in the human astral; Spirits of Fire gave a sort of memory to the etheric; and Sons of Life made the physical express the astral. When the astral was withdrawn during the sun season (paragraph 52 above), Spirits of Form and of Motion, working from the sun, replaced it.

55. The germ of the Spirit Self was formed here. The anthro-poi became able to work more and more like the higher sun beings, and the reunion of the two bodies became possible. The break-away beings became subject to the sun beings. The phys-ical bodies gave up mineral substance, working instead with physical laws in etheric substance. Back in this single body, the Spirits of Motion worked upon the astral and laid the basis of the sentient soul while Spirits of Wisdom working on the etheric body laid the basis of the mind soul, both expressions of the Spirit Self. 56. The other kingdoms were also reabsorbed into the sun, where they also were worked upon by the Spirits of Wisdom. They brought this wisdom with them into the sub-sequent *Earth* incarnation, and we can find it when we study nature closely.

57. The absence of fixed concepts in the description of *Moon* is to give an idea of what actually presents itself to spiritual sight.

58–59. *Moon* evolution, in summary, went through seven cycles, two of preparation, two of closing and three central ones. The high point is the end of the middle (fourth) and beginning of the fifth cycle. Each of these cycles was further divided into seven sections, so there was a total of seven times seven sections. Their divisions were somewhat blurred on *Moon* and even more so on *Sun* and *Saturn*.

Earth

60–61. After a period of withdrawal into higher worlds, the beings developed on *Moon* reemerged in three cycles of *Earth* existence, recapitulations of *Saturn*, *Sun*, and *Moon* in the new conditions. 62. At the end of these three, the beings again withdrew to the spiritual world and higher regions. From there, their descent began in the fourth, our present, cycle of *Earth* existence. 63–64. First, they descended only to have astral form. 65. Then a fireball emerged. Each future human being touched this fireball in only one point. As a result, some of the astral was condensed into a germinal sentient soul, a life body and a physical body of fire. Consciousness remained primarily at the pictorial level.

The following table summarizes material from several paragraphs on the original condition (line 1) and parallel additions to the soul, etheric and physical body.

Soul	Ethers	Elements	Spirits	Paragraph
Sentient	life	fire	Personality	65
Mind	sound	air	Fire	65
Consciousness	light	water	Life	67
I	warmth	solid	human+ Form	71–72, 77

At each further step, the physical body separates successively denser elements—fire, air, water, earth—while the etheric body separates successively denser ethers—life, sound, light, and warmth ethers—until the densest ether is similar to the finest physical element and forces from the physical can be used by the etheric.

66. The earth and sun separated because certain higher beings could not tolerate water in their environment. Henceforth, they work upon earth from outside. 67. The spiritual beings brought about a rotation of the earth around the sun and an alternation in consciousness, with "sleep" occurring during the "day." 68. Something like breathing and digestion appeared in plant-like bodies. As souls returned to their bodies, the dim feeling "This is my form" was the dawning of the I feeling.

Lemuria

69. A solid element was added and incorporated into the bodies, but it was no more dense than smells. Because of this element, the beings were more bound to the surface of the earth, and local influences led to differences in the bodies, a first step toward the differentiation of races. The souls could not just leave these bodies behind during the "days" and return and reenliven them at "night." Rather, the body left behind had to have within it something like a seed containing force for reenlivening it. But when left behind by the souls, physical bodies were hardening more and more so that it was becoming impossible for the souls to reenter them. Soon, souls returning would have found no material with which they could unite. 70. The hardening forces were countered by the separation of the present moon from the earth and the separation of human bodies into different sexes.

71. The Spirits of Form, who had breathed air into the bodies, remained with the "seeds" and guided the returning souls to the right bodies so that the soul developed a memory of these ancestors.

72. The anthropoi experienced their I in warmth currents which became blood circulation and their astral in air shapes which became respiration, while some of the air structures were separated into an organ ancestor to the nervous system. Each anthropos had a mind soul and used it to experience inner images of what was happening outside and to penetrate the delicate nervous system. Liquid and solid structures had to come from the outside under the control of higher beings. Each anthropos felt itself to be an I. It breathed and felt the working of the Spirits of Form. In the streaming warmth worked Spirits of Personality, but behind them were felt the Spirits of Form. The soul said, "Now are working the spirits from whom a spark warms my inner being." The Fire spirits worked in light and gave rise to concepts and memories. With what they received from these spirits, the anthropoi could make the air around them glow. Likewise, the Sons of Life worked in sound and tone. Light, sound, and taste sensations were different at different times in the life cycle.

73. The outer body reflected the inner state. What would later form the head was the most developed. There were three broad groups, those that had been in contact with the fire element and Spirits of Form at the beginning, those that entered at the air stage and worked mainly with the Spirits of Fire, and those that entered at the water stage and worked mainly with the Sons of Life in their inner life. The first group had the most developed heads and most harmonious inner life; the third group had the most developed limbs and strongest impulse for earthly deeds.

74. Before the separation of the sun, Saturn had already separated. Before separation of the moon, Jupiter and Mars also separated to provide for souls not strong enough to transform the increasingly dense human bodies. Moreover, some of the

bodily descendants of humans were so dense that they could receive only souls below the human level. 75. These beings, remnants from the old *Moon*, were ancestors of the animal kingdom. They did not live in individual animals but in all the descendants of one ancestor. A new animal soul embodied only when descendants became quite different from the original. A single group soul belongs to all individuals in a species or genus. 76. Plants originated from a similar process before the separation of the sun.

77. When the consciousness soul had developed an appropriate body, the *Spirits of Form gave that body a spark of their own fire*. The I was released in the body. Humans felt themselves independent in the spiritual world. 78. In the body-free state, they could at first see the sun beings only by reflection in the moon beings.

79. The mineral kingdom represents what remained solid after the moon separated. It also represents the element of human evolution that stayed behind at the *Saturn* stage.

80. The spiritual beings working from the moon would have made human consciousness a mirror of knowledge of the cosmos, but other beings, the rebels from *Moon* evolution, began to make the astral body independent of the higher beings. 81. Humans became masters of their knowledge, but the control originated from the astral, and the I became constantly dependent on this lower element and the *Luciferic* spirits, as they may be called. They gave the anthropoi both the possibility of free activity in consciousness and the possibility of error and evil. 82. The conflict of the sun spirits and the Luciferic spirits made it impossible for the anthropoi to recognize the physical effects of the sun, for the astral—full of the workings of the Luciferic beings—was drawn up into the I. The I then became more entangled in earthly substance than had been intended by the

higher spirits. Bodies grew denser. 83. The spiritual origin of the Luciferic influences explains why they could work so deeply into the bodily nature. 84. Living in accordance with desires, passions, and erroneous, astral-permeated mental images of the outer world brought illness. Having lost awareness of life as a continuation of a body-free existence, the anthropoi now experienced death. 85. A portion of the life body was kept outside the physical so that it could be governed by higher beings, not by the human I. Otherwise, humans would have reincarnated almost immediately after death in their descendants without first reconnecting with the higher spiritual beings. 86. To counterbalance the Luciferic forces working in the astral and the I, all of the higher beings worked in the human etheric and physical during sleep.

87. As a result of this work and the separation of the moon, human bodies were now able to bring back the souls that had moved to other planets (paragraph 74). Individual human karma appeared. Because some of the life body had been removed from the influence of the I, reproduction was unconscious. Logical thinking was elementary, but memory and intuitive knowledge of living beings was highly developed. But knowledge of what the future would bring was lost, and the possibility of fear was implanted. 88. This fear indicated that Ahrimanic beings were at work. 89. The leader of the sun's evolution became the higher I that worked in the life bodies of human souls who had remained with the earth. In this being is revealed to present-day humanity the relation of Christ to the cosmos. The leaders of groups that had gone to other planets also worked as the higher I of those souls as they returned. 90. Lemuria ended in firestorms brought on by abuse of the I spark by souls not well enough protected from the Luciferic influence.

Atlantis

91. During the firestorms, the beings least touched by error retreated to an area presently covered by the Atlantic Ocean. There developed the Atlantean condition. It was the time of actual division into races. It was also a time of strong Luciferic seduction which inclined the soul towards error, especially in the misuse of forces of growth and reproduction. 92. There were, however, oracles, places where the intentions of spiritual beings were perceived. In them worked initiates who tried to eliminate error in their mental work and to discover the original intention of higher beings. Each of these oracles was related to one of the spiritual beings who had once led groups of souls to other planets. Descendants of those who had stayed on the earth were attracted to the Sun oracle, also called the Christ oracle because it was guided by the being who had led the sun from the earth and who would later aid in understanding the Christ. 93. Saturn, Jupiter, and Mars (the outer planets) had left before the separation of the sun. After leaving earth with the sun, further groups of spirits separated forming Venus and Mercury, and these also formed oracles. The first being to separate from the sun after it split from the earth, however, did not form a separate planet but lived in earth's environment. Humans who had absorbed the most Luciferic influence looked to this being and formed the Vulcan oracle. Its initiates began what later became the arts and sciences; Mercury and Venus initiates laid the basis for knowledge of supersensible things. Mercury, Venus and Vulcan initiates all received their inspiration in thoughts while to the outer-planet initiates inspiration came more in symbols. The sun initiates received direct revelations, which they clothed in thoughts.

94. Speech is one result of higher beings turning the Luciferic densification to good ends. Among non-initiates in

late Atlantis, false ideas of reincarnation arose from identifying with the souls of ancestors encountered during sleep. 95. The human physical body was still soft and expressed soul characteristics. Advanced souls had small bodies. The present physical form came about by densification of the Atlantean one.

96. Betrayal of the oracles led to misuse of the ability to manipulate the forces of growth and reproduction and unleashed related forces in air and water, thus producing catastrophes that gradually destroyed Atlantis. Those that did not perish had to emigrate, mostly eastward. Betrayal of the Vulcan mysteries increasingly deprived humanity of a feeling for the spiritual element. Grotesque human forms appeared but died out. Post-Atlantean humans developed from forms already too solidified to succumb to soul forces contrary to nature. 97. From the middle of the Atlantean age, Ahrimanic beings worked to cut off human souls, including those of the dead, from the spiritual world.

98. Amid the general decline, the Sun or Christ oracle preserved the ancient service and was able to recreate the other oracles. 99. In humanity in general, and among the associates of the Christ initiate in particular, the etheric body came to coincide more and more closely with the physical. As a result, they lost their vast memory. But this part of the etheric body also transformed the brain into an instrument for thinking and I-consciousness. The associates of the Sun oracle had the best intellect of the time but the least experience in the supersensible. In the transition to the post-Atlantean condition, the Christ initiate moved with his associates to a secluded area in Central Asia. Under his guidance, copies of the etheric and astral bodies of the greatest Atlantean initiate from each oracle were used to create worthy successors.

The Post-Atlantean Condition

ANCIENT INDIAN EPOCH

These initiates were sent to India, where people particularly valued experiences of the spiritual world and regarded the sense world as *maya*, illusion. They worked as if magically on their disciples. The Christ initiate among them taught in signs and symbols, not in concepts as had the last of his Atlantean predecessors. 101. This Ancient India existed long before the "ancient India" of external history; no external documents of this age survive. 102. At that time, inner memories of ancestors made it easy to understand supersensible teachings but also led to false ideas of reincarnation and, later, to the caste system.

ANCIENT PERSIAN EPOCH

103. In the succeeding Ancient Persian age, people turned their interests more and more to the physical world and became great warriors and artisans. The legacy of supersensible knowledge was used magically for both good and evil. The Luciferic attraction was very strong for these people. 104. It was so strong, in fact, that the guardian of the Sun oracle provided a great leader whose name has come down to us as Zarathustra, or Zoroaster in Greek form. In special states of consciousness, he saw that the sun's leading spirit, who had protected the human life body, would, at a future time, be able to live in a human astral body in the same way that he had lived in the life body since the Luciferic intervention. In contrast to this coming incarnation of the great Sun spirit, the Christ, Zarathustra also pointed to his adversary, Ahriman, who had been active since the betrayal of the Vulcan mysteries.

EGYPTO-CHALDEAN EPOCH

105. Post-Atlantean humanity's task is to develop soul capacities through applying wide-awake thinking and heart forces to active work and observation in the sense world without direct stimulation by the spiritual world. Mastery of the sense world through those capacities is its mission. The Persian peoples began this work but largely with forces remaining from earlier times. The initiates of the Chaldeans and Babylonians saw the natural world as manifestations of spiritual powers. The Egyptians saw the world in need of transformation through their own thought and might. Inspired primarily by the Mercury (or Hermes) oracle led by a reincarnated disciple of Zarathustra, they were able to recognize spiritual laws in the sense-perceptible world. By working in accordance with the intentions of spiritual powers, they hoped to be able to unite with these powers after death.

GRECO-ROMAN EPOCH

106. Initiates of mystery centers were able to rise to high levels of spiritual perception and sought to create a place in the sense world which would express the spiritual element. Thus arose the Greek temple and other art. Greek philosophy and poetry had similar origins in the mysteries.

The Incarnation of the Sun Spirit and the Modern World

107. Interest in the sense world, however, carried with it the danger of regarding it as the only world, and thus falling into the power of Ahriman, who would completely isolate such souls in the life after death. 108. The description earlier in this

book of after-death experiences assumes some degree of victory over Ahriman in this life. 109. Those souls, however, that brought the cultivation of sensory physical existence to full flower thereby condemned themselves to a shadowy existence after death. Thus, the mission of the Greco-Latin epoch necessarily led to estrangement from the spirit and, therefore, to decline. Two streams of initiation opposed this decline. One required inducing special states of soul in which the higher members of anthropos could be seen bearing symbols of the spiritual forces of certain higher beings. The other required the initiates to practice all the capacities the soul had acquired since mid-Atlantean times to an extent far greater than necessary to perceive the sense world. Thereby they were able to behold the creative powers active in the kingdoms of nature below the human, the secrets which Ahriman tries to conceal. But the mysteries could only prophesy the coming of one with an astral body that could become aware of the Sun spirit through the life body without any special soul condition and with a physical body such that all the powers that Ahriman hides would be manifest. For such a being, death can change nothing; in him, the I appears in such a way that the full spiritual being is contained in physical life. 110. Moses, an initiate of both streams, was such a prophet.

111. With the appearance of the Christ, all mystery wisdom had to be reoriented to enable people to recognize in the Christ the Sun spirit who had become human and to understand the natural and physical worlds from this center of wisdom. 112. When His astral body contained all that Lucifer tries to conceal, the Christ became a teacher of the wisdom which will allow attainment of *Earth*'s physical goal. With the event of Golgotha, the force to turn Ahriman's influence to good was implanted in the anthropoi. Henceforth, we can take with us

through death something which frees us from isolation in the spirit world. Not only can we take into the spirit world the spiritual fruits of our work in the sense world, but also on reincarnating we bring to the sense world what the Christ impulse has meant for us in the spirit world. 113. So far, only the smallest part of this wisdom has taken physical effect, but a new ideal for life has been formed. Up until this event, evolution had split humanity into groups. As a result of it, the feeling arose that each inner I has the same origin.

FIFTH AND SIXTH POST-ATLANTEAN EPOCHS

114. The fifth post-Atlantean epoch began in the fifteenth century and continues today. The peoples that carried it forward came from Atlanteans least touched by the preceding epochs. They encountered a matured attraction to the physical world with youthful souls. Hence came their capacity to master the physical world. But hence came also a split within the human soul, one part turned toward the sense world, one toward the spiritual. 115. The sixth epoch must heal this split. To do so, the results of spiritual sight must be grasped and the manifestation of the spirit in the experiences of the sense world must be recognized.

Review Questions

What are the three preceding incarnations of the *Earth*? What sort of beings were present in each? What physical conditions existed? What was the human ancestor like?

What are the nine ranks of spiritual beings? What are their characteristics?

What are the seven stages of consciousness employed here?

How would you characterize each? (The next chapter is also relevant to this question.)

At each preceding planetary stage, the germinal beginning of one of the systems within the present physical body was formed. What were they?

Describe the middle condition of each planetary incarnation when some beings reach "their human stage." What can it mean to "reach the human stage" in such vastly different circumstances?

Where are the origins of Spirit Self, Life Spirit, and Spirit Man to be found? Where are those of sentient soul and mind soul?

What was the revolt during *Moon* all about? How was it dealt with? What are its consequences for today?

Why do we find such wisdom in the world of nature?

What led to the separation into sexes?

Who are the Luciferic and Ahrimanic spirits? How do they differ? How do they oppose one another? How do they cooperate? What works for their redemption?

Why was the sun separated from the earth? Why the moon? What were the consequences of these separations?

How did the mysteries develop during Atlantean times? What were the continuations in the post-Atlantean epochs?

What mystery streams opposed the estrangement from the spirit in Greco-Roman times?

What happened in the Christ event? How does it affect future evolution?

Discussion Questions

What does all this evolution, especially that before the *Earth*, help us to understand?

What is the difference between "physical" and "material" or "mineral"?

What evidence do you see that the physical is the oldest, most perfect human member?

Is it logical to assert that we are beings of spiritual origin and yet our physical body is our oldest and most perfect member?

What do we owe to the various rebellious spirits?

What was the nature of the "Fall of anthropos?"

Christian teachers have struggled for nearly two thousand years with the relation of the human and the divine in the incarnated Christ. It is a perhaps presumptuous question, but how do you see that matter in the light of this chapter?

In the brief time since the incarnation of the Sun spirit, the Christ, many things have changed. Human consciousness has profoundly changed, as you can quickly verify by reading any medieval author. Where in these changes do you believe that you see the working of the Christ? In particular, what would be the connection of the Christ—not necessarily of organized Christianity—with the rise of science in its widest sense?

Observations

This chapter will take us not merely through the evolution of the earth as we usually think of it but through three of its previous incarnations, incarnations of which not one physical scrap, no fossil, no rock, no mineral deposit remains. One may well then ask, Of what conceivable interest or use is such a story? But the answer is easy. Just as we cannot understand the individual by looking at only one incarnation, so can we not understand the earth and our species from a single incarnation. If we seek to understand why we have not just an I but also an astral body, an etheric body, and a physical body, we must look back to these earlier incarnations of the earth to find their origins. Thus, the science of these "manifest secrets" demands this study.

In the course of this chapter, Steiner will explain the origins of these three bodies from the workings of spiritual beings. Matter is always result, never primal cause. In this way, the *theory* of evolution presented here is diametrically opposed to the theory taught in most classrooms and texts on evolution. By contrast, there is little difference in the *facts*, except of course for the enormous increase in the range and perspective offered here. But fossils and the careful reconstruction of past geological epochs are welcome evidence in Steiner's account.

Since this evidence is also used by the conventional, matter-first school of evolution, one may wonder how it is possible that this school, with all its well-funded, meticulous research could so completely miss the point of the facts it has so well documented. The answer seems to lie in the descent of human consciousness to the point where the very idea of a spiritual being has become unknown and unwelcome. Darwin faced criticism from the religious side which could no more see a spiritual being in the *yom*, or "day," of the Genesis account than he could—in fact, in the case of Darwin himself, probably less. Today's evolutionists contend with "fundamentalist" opposition which, in the name of religion, puts forward a very materialist interpretation of a profoundly spiritual document, the book of Genesis. Evolutionists have become so sensitive on the point that any criticism of the standard position put forward from outside their ranks is just denounced as totally unscientific.

Today, one who has not looked into the matter for himself or herself is apt to feel rather comfortably that the "standard" theory of evolution fits all the facts and works at least as well as Newtonian mechanics does for the solar system. In fact, nothing could be further from the truth. In the first place there is the philosophical problem of the tautology in the "modern synthesis" of evolutionary theory, that is, it seems to make a statement that is true by definition, something like "the survivors survive." According to this synthesis, evolution happens because there is random, chance mutation in genetic material producing ever new forms; and from among these forms natural selection picks those that are fit to survive. Now we say that something is random when we have no explanation for it. And as for what is fit, well, what survives is fit. So the theory becomes survival of the survivors from among forms whose origin we do not try to explain. Clearly, there can be no counterexample of the being that survived despite the fact that it was unfit or was fit but nonetheless perished. Nor can there be any form which could not by some wild chance have originated from some other form. Thus the theory in its modern form is neither testable nor "scientific" in the textbook definition of that term.

Steiner's "theory," by contrast, not only proposes a vastly different moving force but calls upon a different method of proof, as we have seen above. In my own experience, it meets this method of proof, while the conventional theory fails this test and degenerates into a tautology relative to its own standards of proof.

Darwin's original theory was not tautology. He expected small changes to build into big ones; he expected gradual change. As beautifully and dispassionately documented by Michael Denton in *Evolution: a Theory in Crisis* (Adler & Adler, Bethesda, Md., 1986), this theory has proven a half-truth. While it explains well enough micro-evolution—such as that of the change in color of the peppered moth in England or the differentiation of a group of lizards in the Caribbean—it has yet to produce any case of macro-evolution. There is literally no case where one species of a decidedly "higher," more conscious order has been shown to have developed from a "lower" order. I once spent two days in intense study of the fossils in the Natural History Museum in Vienna, a large museum with its collections laid out in phylogenetic order for the benefit of the scholar rather than the tourist. At the end, I was completely awed both by the variety of life and by the absence of intermediate forms. All the links were missing. Darwin's view of gradual evolution of lower into higher forms had no example that I could find to support it. (In the examples of micro-evolution, such as in the Caribbean lizards, the fundamental factor responsible for it usually seems to be isolation, not struggle for existence.)

Darwin was aware, of course, of this problem, and blamed the fragmentary nature of the fossil record. As more and more fossils have been collected and cataloged, the problem has remained but Darwin's explanation has become less and less plausible. Indeed, its explanation has become a major concern of modern evolutionary theory. The theory of punctuated equilibria of N. Eldredge and S. J. Gould, while offering a plausible explanation of the gaps between species of the same genus, can hardly explain the much larger gaps between genera or families. Indeed, the main effect of this theory seems to have been to call public attention to the gaps. (See Denton, *Evolution...*, pp. 192–195.)

Other expectations derived from the theory have proven mistaken. When molecular biology provided a measure of distance between species, it was confidently expected that the traditionally taught evolutionary series cyclostome →fish → amphibian → reptile →mammal would be clearly demonstrable. Incredibly, there is not a trace of it. In the molecular structure of their genes, humans are as close to lampreys (a cyclostome) as are fish! (Denton, p. 284) The fauna of the Burgess Shale, from about the first third of the Cambrian period and therefore at the dawn of the fossil record, show greater—not less—diversity in fundamental forms or phyla than all the fossils of all subsequent eras. This material has been vividly presented for the layman by Stephen Jay Gould in *Wonderful Life* (Norton, New York, 1989). Gould, a leading Darwinist, frankly admits that these discoveries were not what he or others were expecting and, indeed, that expectations had initially unintentionally distorted the presentation of the evidence. He seems, however, to miss the point that such variety at such an early time must point to extensive and rapid evolution in preceding soft forms which did not leave fossils. Steiner, in fact, points clearly to these soft forms and to their highly varied evolution. The Burgess Shale fits perfectly in the picture described by Steiner.

A typical fallacy in evolutionary thinking is represented in a recent article by Richard Dawkins in *Nature* (vol. 368, April 21, 1994, pp. 690–1). Dawkins reports a computer experiment on the evolution of the shape of eye. The program started from a computer representation of a flat light-sensitive disk, allowed only one-percent changes in the shape in random directions in any one step and accepted only steps that increased the refractive index. Some 300 random steps were sufficient to produce a well-shaped eye with a good refractive index. Dawkins calculates that in real time these 300 steps might require some 400,000 years, just the twinkling of an eye in geological time. What he forgets is that the experimenters supplied the measure of improvement, the refractive index. What the experiment demonstrates is that when there is present the consciousness of a spiritual being which can take advantage of an organ of a particular type, random variation and selection for improvement can fairly quickly produce it. In this case, the spiritual consciousness was that of the experimenter who supplied the formula for the refractive index and the rule to accept only steps that improved it. What Dawkins wants to argue is that no spiritual being is necessary; what the experiment shows is the opposite.

Finally, if survival is the point of evolution, it is hard to see why it ever got past the arthropod stage, for the variety and hardiness of the insects far exceeds that of the vertebrates, not to mention the fragile existence of the mammals. If, however, development of vehicles for consciousness by spiritual beings was the object, then evolution begins to make sense.

In short, Steiner's presentation in this chapter is in no way counter to the facts pointing to evolution. It does, however, make far better sense of them than does the conventional theory.

§

Steiner makes extensive use in this chapter of the four elements—fire, air, water, earth—and four ethers—life, sound, light, warmth—both listed in order of increasing density. The four elements are found in writings of Empedocles and Aristotle. For Aristotle, the elements were found below the moon sphere while above it there was a "fifth essence," the *aithér*. For Homer, the *aithér* was the pure upper air, the home of the gods, while *aér* was the air we mortals breathe. For Aristotle, the main property of the *aithér* was "always to run"—*aei thein*—to run like the rim of potter's wheel runs round and round (*De caelo*, A 3, 270b 22). He saw this property, of course, in the continual motion of the heavenly bodies. He may have felt a consonance between the words *aithér* and *aei thein*. Aristotle held, in contrast to Empedocles, that the elements could be transformed into one another—a process important in Steiner's description.

Needless to say, these elements were replaced by others in the history of chemistry, while the lower three became "states." Steiner is not trying to turn back the clock in science, however. Rather, he is pointing out that these four elements and ethers can be very helpful in making sense of the world around us in ways which go beyond what material science is able to do. As so often in the book, the proof of the validity of the concept is its ability to help us see to the heart of matters which would otherwise remain opaque.

§

8. *Akasha* (or *akasa*—but with the *s* pronounced as palatized *sh*) is one of the five elements in Sankhya philosophy and is identified with space, ether, or sky. Steiner is not the only reader of this akashic record. It was, for example, also the source of the account of creation given in Genesis and, quite likely, in other sources. One may wonder how "reading" of the same source gives rise to such divergent reports. I am reminded, however, of an occasion some years ago when four of us who had been in Russia during the summer were asked to talk about our experiences to the Russian club at the university. We had had very different experiences, and the students commented that they could hardly believe that we had all been to the same country. We who had been there, however, were struck by how each of the reports rang true and faithfully reflected the country we had been in! The fact that different reports of the akashic record sound as different as this book and Genesis only means that the observers

were very different. In contrast to earlier observers, Steiner presents an account in concepts instead of mythic images. Note also that it is quite possible for the reporter to err in the interpretation of what has been seen. The seer's logical and interpretative capacities are no more infallible than anyone else's. The occurrence of such errors does not, however, necessarily mean that the seer did not see.

12. It may help to remember the names of the earlier incarnations of the *Earth* to note that they follow the days of the week—Satur(n)day, Sunday and Mo(o)nday. The same is true for the two following incarnations, *Jupiter* and *Venus* (described in chapter 6), though we have to go to one of the romance languages, say Italian, to see it in *Jiovedi* and *Veneredi*.

17. The remarkable little passage about damage to the astral body producing illness in the next incarnation is elaborated in the lectures in *Manifestations of Karma* (Hamburg, May 1910, GA 120), especially lecture 4. A weak feeling of I in one life will lead to the desire to encounter the greatest possible opposition to the I in the next incarnation so that this I can strengthen itself in meeting that opposition. In that subsequent incarnation, the I may seek out, subconsciously of course, a cholera epidemic. Cholera produces violent vomiting and dehydration so that the blood, the particular organ of the I, becomes very thick and offers the maximum resistance to penetration by the I. (The ratio of the red blood cells to the serum, as seen in blood sedimentation tests, becomes very high.) An overbearing I in one life, on the other hand, may seek the opposite condition, such as is offered by malaria, a disease that breaks down red blood cells producing a very low ratio of cells to serum or a thin blood. Further examples are found in *Karmic Relationships*, vol 1, (Dornach, 1924, lecture 5, GA 235). One who has little

interest in the physical surrounding world will be weakly in the next incarnation, while one "bursting with health" certainly had a keen interest in the visible world in a former incarnation. Lack of interest in the stars in one life leads to a limp and flabby body in the next life; lack of interest in music will lead to asthmatic trouble in the next life.

21. The distinction Steiner makes between physical and mineral is important and, indeed, generally accepted. Physics studies many "things" which have no material existence—force, energy, gravitation, magnetic fields, electric fields, light, radiant heat, and so on. Indeed, most of physics seems to be about non-material subjects which, nonetheless, obey physical laws.

The spiritual beings introduced in this paragraph will be with us throughout this chapter, and indeed, throughout much of Steiner's work. He gives them names to denote their essences but also uses the traditional names given them by Dionysios the Areopagite in his *The Hierarchies of Angels and of the Church*. This work, given its present form somewhere between 430 and 530, probably represents a tradition descending from Paul's convert, Dionysios the Areopagite, mentioned in Acts 17:32. Four of these names appear in order in Paul's letter to the Ephesians, 1:21: "far above all principality and power and might and dominion" (in Greek "*hyperanó pasés archés kai exousias kai dynameós kai kyriotétos*"). Paul is, in fact, placing the Christ being in the heavenly hierarchies. Below these four appear the angels and archangels and above them, the thrones, cherubim, and seraphim, in ascending order. Dionysios is able to tell us disappointingly little about these beings; he just gives a little meditation on the name of each.

The complete system is:

Spirits of:	Dionysios:	English:
First Hierarchy		
Love	Seraphim	Seraphim
the Harmonies	Cherubim	Cherubim
Will	Thrones	Thrones
Second Hierarchy		
Wisdom	Kyriotetes	Dominions
Motion	Dynamis	Mights or Virtues
Form	Exousiai	Powers
Third Hierarchy		
Personality	Archai	Principalities
Fire	Archangeloi	Archangels
Life or Twilight	Angeloi	Angels

Besides these names, Steiner at times refers to the *Exousiai* by their Hebrew name of *Elohim*, while the *Archai* are the *Yamim* (or "days") of Genesis. (In *Cosmic Memory* Steiner uses the terms "Principalities" for the Spirits of Motion or *Dynamis* and "Primal beginnings" for the Spirits of Personality or *Archai*. The second is a literal translation of the Greek, but the first is a confusing mistake. For some unknown reason, Steiner or his editors spelled *Exousiai* as "*Exusiai*," and this spelling is found in many anthroposophic sources. The Greek is *exousiai*, so to write "exusiai" is like spelling the Greek word for mind, *nous*, as *nus*, which is certainly not the usual practice in English. The Creeger translation adopted the standard English transliteration as "exousiai," and I have followed this good example.)

Learning these names *in order* is the key for making sense of the rest of this chapter. You will note also that each hierarchy has a distinct character which begins to become apparent in this paragraph. To learn the order, you may try a mnemonic like, "Let's hope Will wisely moves forward past free lunches," but once you have the characters in mind you won't need it. Further accounts of these beings can be found in Steiner's lecture courses such as *Universe, Earth and Man* (1908, GA 105), *The Spiritual Hierarchies and the Physical World* (1909, GA 110), and *The Spiritual Beings in the Heavenly Bodies and in the Kingdoms of Nature* (1912, GA 136).

You may find these hierarchies depicted in many places in Christian art, for example, at the top of the ceiling of the baptistery in Florence, where they preside over the unfolding of human history below them, or rising majestically on the rood screen of the Episcopal National Cathedral in Washington.

Besides the hierarchies, there is another sequence which you will need to keep in mind, that of states of consciousness. Here are the seven that concern us here, from lowest to highest, lined up with the beings which currently have them as a normal state.

Consciousness	Being	Awareness
Mineral	Minerals	Response to heat or chemicals
Deep sleep	Plants	Growth and nutrition
Pictorial	Animals	Pictures but no I awareness
Object	Humans	I and external objects
Imaginative	Angel	Images of spiritual beings
Inspirational	Archangels	Words of spiritual beings
Intuitive	Archai	Inner essence of spiritual beings

The hierarchies each move up one level with each incarnation of the planet. The one which has an object consciousness while working in the physical element is said to be at its "human" stage, or better, at the stage comparable to that of present humans.

22. On each successive planetary incarnation the next lower hierarchy will go through its "human" stage. On *Earth*, it is, of course, we who do so. What does it mean to go through the human stage? It seems to have to do with consciousness, with having an awareness of the I. Lower stages are the dream-like consciousness of present-day animals or the dreamless-sleep consciousness of plants. Higher stages are the imaginative, inspirational, and intuitive consciousness described in chapter 5.

24. The combination of inner taste and outward music in the seventh stage of *Saturn* may seem strange. When we come later to the different ethers we will find, however, that one and the same ether may be called either the sound ether or the chemical ether. One connection between the two appears in the importance of combinations in integral proportions in both harmony and chemistry.

25. Steiner speaks here of the consciousness of minerals. We normally think of them as unconscious, but how do we ascertain whether another being has consciousness? Clearly, by seeing whether it will respond to some sort of stimulus. Now the minerals certainly respond to external stimuli and in precise and dependable ways. In the expansion of metals and gases with heat, the freezing and evaporation of water at precise temperatures, or in the orderly crystallization processes, their consciousness becomes evident. Indeed, without the surprising but precise behavior of water, life as we know it would be totally impossible. You may, of course, say that this consciousness is mechanical—indeed, that is just what Steiner called it.

Matters get more complicated on the *Sun* and we need a bit of "celestial mechanics" to keep straight what is going on. First of all, there are two bodies, physical and etheric, to be worked on; and secondly, the periods of activity are divided into two parts. It is as if we were at a conference in Spain lasting seven days, including the evenings. We work during the mornings until about two o'clock, then break for *almuerzo* and siesta, reconvene in the cool of the evening and begin a new subject with a new speaker. We will work on it until *cena* and bedtime, take it into the spiritual world with us during sleep, and continue it the next morning up until lunch time. Thus, each subject except the first and last overlap two days. This beginning of a period of activity in the evening calls to mind the Jewish practice of beginning the Sabbath and festivals on the evening before the calendar day. This practice, in turn, reflects Genesis 1:5, "... and there was evening and there was morning, one day."

Now the fundamental principle is that a group of spirit beings starts work on the physical body in the evening of one day, continues in the morning of the next, then moves up to the etheric body in the evening and continues there during the next morning.

This schedule is not laid out specifically in this book or in *Cosmic Memory,* and not every combination in it is noted in either book, but whenever you find a reference in either book to who is working where when, it fits this schedule. These references are especially clear in *Cosmic Memory*, pages 184–195. For *Saturn*, we would have had Spirits of Will in the "morning" of the first cycle, then Spirits of Wisdom in the evening of that cycle and the morning of the second, and so on. With this arrangement, it works out in all four incarnations that whatever hierarchy is working in the physical on the "evening" of the fourth cycle reaches its "human" stage at that point, that is, it has a consciousness comparable to ours at present.

Thus for *Sun* we have the following "schedule":

Cycle	Half	Physical	Etheric
1	morning	Wisdom	
	evening	Motion	Wisdom
2	morning	Motion	Wisdom
	evening	Form	Motion
3	morning	Form	Motion
	evening	Personality	Form
4	morning	Personality	Form
	evening	Fire	Personality
5	morning	Fire	Personality
	evening	Twilight	Fire
6	morning	Twilight	Fire
	evening	Human	Twilight
7	morning	Human	Twilight
	evening	Human	Human

39. *Moon* proceeds along a plan similar to that of *Sun*, but with one more body, the astral.

Here is the schedule:

Cycle	Half	Physical	Etheric	Astral
1	morning	Motion		
	evening	Form	Motion	
2	morning	Form	Motion	
	evening	Personality	Form	Motion
3	morning	Personality	Form	Motion
	evening	Fire	Personality	Form
4	morning	Fire	Personality	Form
	evening	Twilight	Fire	Personality
5	morning	Twilight	Fire	Personality
	evening	Human	Twilight	Fire
6	morning	Human	Twilight	Fire
	evening	Human	Human	Twilight
7	morning	Human	Human	Twilight
	evening	Human	Human	Human

This schedule is quite clear in *Cosmic Memory* (see especially chapter xvi), but is detectable also here.

42. The rebellion is described in much more detail in lecture 10 of *The Spiritual Hierarchies and the Physical World.* The rebels were Mights, Spirits of Motion, or Dynamis. And they were acting on commands from higher beings to promote evolution; yet at the same time, they were the originators of evil.

59. At the very end of the *Moon* description, Steiner mentions that each of the seven cycles had been subdivided into seven sections, and mentions that such sections were present on *Sun* and *Saturn* also, although more blurred. These seven sub-cycles have played no role in the previous exposition, which mentioned instead the two-part, "morning-evening" division. In the exposition of *Earth*, the two-part division will disappear; and the seven-part division will become central. This progression from two to seven may be seen as a gradual building of the macro plan into the micro plan, perhaps a result of the working of the Spirits of Wisdom.

Note that at the end of *Moon* evolution, we have laid the foundations for both the lower part of our being—the three bodies—and the higher part, Spirit Self, Life Spirit, and Spirit Man. During the *Earth* evolution, they must come together.

The "celestial mechanics" is less in evidence in *Earth* than in the earlier incarnations, but nonetheless works. We would expect three cycles of repetitions. They are clearly pointed out in paragraph 61. In the first half of the fourth cycle we should find that the Spirits of Form give the I to anthropos. Paragraph 77 describes this event on schedule. Seemingly, the action of the rebels from the *Moon* evolution, who reappear here as Luciferic spirits, required maximum intervention of higher beings in the physical and etheric bodies, as will be described at the end of paragraph 86, so that the orderly sequence of the intervention of the higher hierarchies becomes confused. A passage from *Cosmic Memory* (chapter xvii) adds considerable detail to the

Moon recapitulation and the early stages of the fourth *Earth* cycle. It describes specific connections of higher beings with the bodies, but they seem to be rushed one cycle ahead, so that the Fire Spirits are in the astral, the Sons of Life in the etheric, and humans in the physical, as they should be in the second half of the fourth cycle, not the second half of the third cycle as indicated in the text. Have I missed a count? Did Steiner slip? Or is it an effect of the Luciferic beings pushing things ahead too fast?

Cosmic Memory also helps with names of various ages. *An Outline of Esoteric Science* indicates three cycles of recapitulation (paragraph 60 and 61) and does not indicate further names of periods until paragraph 91, where the names Hyperborea, Lemuria, and Atlantis are introduced, the first two referring to ages covered previously in the chapter but not easily identified. In discussing this material, it is convenient to have names—and Steiner often used them in his lectures—so let us borrow them from *Cosmic Memory* and try to relate them to the present book. Within this fourth cycle of *Earth* evolution, we find four successive "states of development," sometimes called "globes." These are:

Arupa—formless, when the densest things are comparable to the highest human thought, mathematical or moral. Animals, for example, exist only as states of consciousness of Spirits of Fire. The human Spirit Man, Life Spirit, and Spirit Self exist in the consciousness of the Spirits of Form.

Rupa—formed, when the density does not yet exceed that of normal thought. Animals become independent thought beings. The human independent thought body is clothed by the Spirits of Form in a body of coarser, formed thought substance.

Astral—humans and animals get astral bodies.

Physical—at first humans consist of a formless thought core, a formed thought body, an astral body, and an etheric body.

We are currently in this fourth "globe" within the fourth *Earth* cycle. This globe is then further subdivided into seven "principal conditions" of which we are the fifth. These five are:

Polarean—the etheric was the densest element. Reproduction of body and soul by division.

Hyperborean—etheric takes on physical bodies of warmth and gradually denser material. Reproductive organs appear. Separation of the sun.

Lemurian—further densification threatens extinction. Extrusion of the moon and subsequent repopulation of the earth. Brought to an end by firestorms.

Atlantean—seven successive ages, ending with destruction by water.

Present—again seven successive ages, of which we are in the fifth, the earlier ones being Indian, Persian, Egypto-Chaldean, and Greco-Roman.

It is hazardous but perhaps helpful to line up particular paragraphs with particular names. The borders are not always distinct, so there is some uncertainty in the following alignment.

Paragraph	*Time period*
62	Arupa and Rupa globes
63–64	Astral globe
65+	Beginning of physical globe, which continues to the end of the chapter.
65	Polarean condition
66–68	Hyperborean condition
69–86	Lemurian condition
87–90	Transition to Atlantis. Steiner's reference in 87 to his essay "Our Atlantean Ancestors" confirms the impression from the content that the paragraph is about Atlantis. The intervention of the Ahrimanic beings in 88 is seemingly placed in mid Atlantean times in 109. But the end of Lemuria in firestorms is not recorded until 90.
91–98	Atlantean condition
99+	Post-Atlantean condition
99–102	Ancient Indian
103–104	Ancient Persian
105	Egypto-Chaldean
106–113	Greco-Roman
114	Modern
114	Sixth

62. The connection of the events chronicled here with the description in Genesis is pinpointed by Steiner in *Genesis, Secrets of the Bible Story of Creation* (August 1910, GA 122, lecture 1).

> Let us concentrate on this moment, when the sun with-
> draws from its former state of union with the rest of the
> planet and begins to send its forces to the earth from
> without.... If we fix this moment firmly in our minds, we
> have the point of time at which Genesis, the creation story,
> begins. This is what it is describing. We should not associ-
> ate with the opening words of Genesis the abstract, shad-
> owy idea we get when we say "In the beginning" which is
> something unspeakably poverty-stricken compared with
> what the ancient Hebrew sage felt....

The lecture cycle continues with an explanation of what the Hebrew words called forth in the minds of their hearers. It also identifies the *Elohim* (translated as God in the English versions, though the form is plainly plural) with the Spirits of Form. The famous seven "days" (*Yamim*) are seven spiritual beings, Spirits of Personality, who guide the successive processes. The connec-tion of spiritual beings with days is deeply rooted. Consider the names of the days of the week; Tuesday, Wednesday, Thursday and Friday are, respectively, Tyr's day (god of war), Odin's day, Thor's day, and Freyja's day. The similarity of *deus* (god) and *dies* (day) in Latin is not accidental. There are ancient statues of aeons as divine beings. In the mosaics of one of the domes of the narthex of St. Mark's in Venice, you will see the days of creation as beings robed in white and lined up beside one another.

In these lectures, Steiner comments that in writing *An Out-line of Esoteric Science* he deliberately avoided pointing out any parallels to Genesis because he wished to be quite clear that what was written lived before his own spiritual eye. It was in no way dependent on Genesis or any other external document. If we may take that point as now well established, I will at several places below follow his own example in pointing out parallels between what is written here and in Genesis. Many more are in these lectures.

70. The separation into sexes is described in much more detail in *Cosmic Memory*, chapter vi. In natural science, there are basically three theories of the origin of the moon, referred to as the daughter, sister, and wife theories. The daughter theory is that described here, to which used to be added that the moon came out where the Pacific now is. The sister theory says that the earth and moon were formed as separate bodies in the same original process. The wife theory says that the moon was formed somewhere far away, came flying by, and got caught by the earth's gravitation. When the moon rocks proved much older than the Pacific, that part of the daughter theory had to be dropped. At the same time, the moon explorations gave other evidence supporting the daughter theory but with a very early separation date at the time of the forming of the earth's core. (See *The Cambridge Encyclopedia of Earth Sciences*, [Crown, New York, 1981] page 58.) One must, however, reserve judgement on any issue involving radioactive dating, as these do. It is based upon a decay process which is assumed to progress at a constant rate throughout all time. But with living bodies, such assumptions can be tricky. For example, "In 1982, Bill was six feet and one quarter inches tall; in 1992, he was six feet exactly. How tall was Bill in 1492?" Bill is clearly a gentleman over sixty, but not over 500! To the extent that the earth is a much more living body than is the moon, which had hardened, according to Steiner, much earlier than the earth, radioactive dates derived from moon material may put a given event further back than do dates based on earth material.

71. This paragraph recapitulates earlier paragraphs with slightly different emphasis. The parallel with Genesis 2:7 is striking: "And the Lord God formed man out of the dust of the

ground and breathed into his nostrils the breath of life; and man became a living soul."

Note carefully the use of "dust," the finest possible form of the earth element. With this meaning of "dust, the passage "... for dust thou art, and unto dust shalt thou return" (Genesis 3:19) seems almost to promise an ultimate respiritualization. The phenomenon of memory, of an I that flowed down through the generations, appears in Genesis as the patriarchs that live hundreds of "years." These years may, in fact, be the generations. Indeed, Genesis 5 begins with the words: "This is the book of the generations of Adam."

73. Note the curious absence of the Spirits of Personality in this sequence of spiritual beings.

75–76. The mention of animals and plants in these paragraphs raises two questions: (1) How does all of Steiner's description relate to conventional geologic time and (2) What is our relation to the animals?

Relative to geological time, Steiner wisely avoided dates. The conventionally accepted dates at the time he was writing were far different from those currently accepted. Any dates which he might have given, had they seemed reasonable to his contemporaries, would mark him as "dated" today. On the other hand, the qualitative geological ages have remained fairly stable since they were first identified in the early nineteenth century. Rough qualitative matching of some of Steiner's descriptions is possible. Of the Lemurian age, he writes in *Cosmic Memory* (chapter v):

> The air was much thicker even than in later Atlantean times, the water much thinner. And what forms the firm crust of our earth today was not yet as hard as it later became. The world of plants and animals had developed

only as far as the amphibians, the birds, and the lower mammals, and as far as vegetable growths which resemble our palms and similar trees.

The plant and animal life sounds like a Paleocene landscape. The omission of reptiles probably means that it is not Cretaceous, when they would have been too evident to omit. Atlantis, on the other hand, is thought to coincide fairly closely with the Pleistocene.

Our relation with the animals is more complicated. On the one hand it is perfectly clear that, as spiritual beings, we are not descended from them. As spiritual beings, our divine spark was given us by the Spirits of Form. The animals are, however, our bodily cousins. From paragraph 75, they seem to have taken over forms abandoned by human souls. In the development of new forms, we—working in forms too soft to leave any fossils—were the pioneers, and they took what we could no longer use. We should thus expect to be able to see in the animal phyla an image, much transformed to be sure, of our own past. Hermann Poppelbaum's *A New Zoology* (Philosophic-Anthroposophic Press, Dornach, 1961) is a remarkable, systematic effort to read the animal forms in this way. The fact of the Cambrian explosion in which virtually all phyla appear all at once in the fossil record was made all the more impressive by the reconstruction of the Burgess Shale fauna described above. It would seem unambiguously to point to the soft-form evolution. The discovery in recent years of Precambrian macro-fossils in the Ediacara Hills of Australia points in the same direction. For these animals, fossilized in exceptionally perfect conditions in fine sand, come to us only in molds and casts—imprints in the sand. They had beautiful bodies of some size but all too soft to leave any trace of their own bodily material in ideal conditions. If evolution in soft forms is the key to understanding the Cambrian explosion, may it not also be the key to understanding the upward development of more and more conscious animal forms?

As humans experimented with soft forms and, after a while, abandoned them, they were taken up by animal group souls that needed just such bodies. And suddenly, the fossil record shows a new, more highly conscious creature. Meanwhile, of course, densification and diversification of already living beings proceeds. This view of evolution does not deny a role to Darwinism, but provides the drive towards more and more conscious, more human-like beings which it lacks. Steiner's emphasis on the thicker air, thinner water, and softer earth in the passage quoted above is quite relevant to the viability of these soft forms.

Soft forms, however, do not seem to be the whole story from Steiner's observations. There seems to be a definite relation between human spirits and animal bodies. We find

> ... when the sun had just gone forth from the earth, the highest animal form was the fish, although not the fish of today. The form of the animals of that time was entirely different from that of the present fishes, but it stood at the same stage.... Something singular now came about. Certain of the primitive fish-forms remained animals and troubled themselves no further about the progress of evolution. Others, however, retained a certain relation to the human shapes in the following way.... Whenever [a gaseous] human form was on the sunny side [of the earth], there was organized into this gas mass something of such an animal form below in the water earth. Human and animal forms were combined so that there was a human form above and an animal form below.... There were ever higher animal

forms which man took into himself. (*Egyptian Myths and Mysteries*, September 9, 1908, GA 106, lecture 7)

Steiner says nothing about it, but I can imagine the human half of this combination ducking down into the animal half, looking out at the world, and pulling out again. Here we see a definite force for uplift in the animal bodies. Does there come a point when the human ducks down and stays down?

Simultaneously with its first incarnation in the Lemurian Age, the untarnished human spirit, consisting of Atma-Buddhi-Manas [Spirit Man, Life Spirit, and Spirit Self], sought its primal physical incarnation. The physical development of the earth with its animal-like creatures had not evolved so far at that time, the whole of this animal-human organism was not so far advanced then that it could have incorporated the human spirit. But a part of it, *a certain group of animal-like beings had evolved so far that the seed of the human spirit could descend into it to give form to the human body.* (*The Temple Legend*, lecture 1, May 23, 1904, GA 93).

Such a body would be likely to have animal characteristics which would be gradually lifted up by the working of the human members in it.

In still more remote times, the Atlantean clairvoyant could look back to a period when man's physical form was yet more animal-like, though he possessed an etheric body which was entirely human, far more beautiful indeed than the present physical form. (*Universe, Earth and Man*, GA 105, lecture 1)

Thus, it appears, we have indeed cooperated with the animals in the development of both their bodies and ours. We gave them forms we could no longer use. Then, later perhaps, we worked with them to lift up their bodies. Then came a time when we entered some of those bodies more completely. Thereupon, we seem to have begun working the bodies into softer, more youthful forms, through the presence of the human etheric. This factor, not a struggle for existence, has led from animal-like ancestors to today's humanity.

81. The transformation of consciousness as a result of the action of the Luciferic beings calls to mind the eating of the fruit of the tree of consciousness of good and evil. What gives independence gives the possibility of error.

84. In former ages, humans slipped out of earthly skins leaving a "seed" behind in the body by which it could be reenlivened and reentered. Passing between the incarnated and excarnated conditions was not particularly traumatic. Through the influence of the Luciferic beings, however, that all changes. First, we lose consciousness of life as a continuation of body-free existence. Then our runaway astral with its passions, desires, and astral-penetrated mental images leads us to behavior that destroys our bodies. Our spirits then must leave these destroyed bodies in ignorance of what lies beyond. And thus we have the picture of death as we know it, often the culmination of a painful process, and with no direct knowledge of what comes next.

85. This separation of a part of the life body and its removal from the Luciferic influence lest the human spirit should be almost constantly incarnated for me calls to mind the enigmatic Genesis passage: "and now, lest the man put forth his hand and take also of the tree of life, and eat, and live forever: Therefore the Lord God sent him forth from the Garden of Eden ..." (Genesis 3:22–23). Is there a connection here?

87. Most of the descriptions of this paragraph appear to apply to Atlantis in its early to middle periods.

88. The name Ahriman, as indicated in paragraph 97, is taken from the Zoroastrian religion. Steiner frequently referred to the story of Isis and Osiris and always in the form given it by Plutarch in his essay by that name. In that essay, Plutarch also wrote:

> The great majority and the wisest of men hold this opinion: they believe that there are two gods, rivals as it were, the one the Artificer of good and the other of evil. There are also those who call the better one a god and the other a daemon, as, for example, Zoroaster the sage, who, they record, lived five thousand years before the time of the Trojan War. He called the one Oromadzes and the other Areimanion.... Oromadzes may be compared to light, and Areimanion, conversely, to darkness and ignorance, and midway between the two is Mithras. (*Isis and Osiris,* 370A; translation from the Loeb Classical Library edition, Harvard University Press, Cambridge, MA, 1932)

Paragraph 97 also indicates that the Ahrimanic influence enters in the middle of the Atlantean period. The earlier story of these beings is here only hinted at. They "had become abnormal much earlier in the course of evolution than the Luciferic powers." Something more is told in *Manifestations of Karma*, lecture 7 (GA 120).

> These beings who played the same part with regard to the Angeloi that today the Luciferic beings play with regard to ourselves were the Ahrimanic beings which, during the whole of the *Sun* evolution, remained behind as did the

Luciferic beings during the *Moon* evolution. That is why we can only indirectly encounter these beings. It was Ahriman who, as it were, acted as a tempter within the breast of the Angeloi [on *Moon*].

The opposition of Ahriman and Lucifer is the subject of many lectures. The one just cited is a good starting point for study.

ATLANTIS

The classic account is in Plato's *Timaeus* and *Critias*. In the first, an Egyptian priest speaking to Solon places the founding of Athens 9000 years earlier, or about 9600 B.C. Then, after "many great and wonderful deeds," Athens led the defense of the eastern Mediterranean against an invader from "out of the Atlantic Ocean, for in those days the Atlantic was navigable." Atlantis was defeated,

> but afterwards there occurred violent earthquakes and floods; and in a single day and night of misfortune all your warlike men in a body sank into the earth, and the island of Atlantis in like manner disappeared in the depths of the sea. For which reason the sea in those parts is impassable and impenetrable, because there is a shoal of mud in the way; and this was caused by the subsidence of the island. (*Timaeus* 25, B. Jowett tr., Macmillan, London, 1892)

Note particularly the mud in the priest's own time, about 600 B.C. This passage does not date the sinking of Atlantis, only the founding of Athens, so the sinking of Atlantis could be much later. In the *Critias*, however, the priest gives the same date, 9,000 years before his time, for the war, which is not inconsistent if the priest meant to be giving dates accurate only to within 500 years or so.

In *Plato Prehistorian* (Lindisfarne Press, Hudson, NY, 1990), Mary Settegast writes, on the basis of archaeological findings,

> As things now stand, it is 8500 B.C. in uncorrected carbon-14-years that saw a coincidence of events which resemble nothing so much as a war involving all those who lived inside the Straits of Gibraltar.... For all its questionable exotica, this fragmented old tale may be our most reliable guide to the Epi-Paleolithic Old World.

Settegast then uses Plato's account as a framework for understanding a mass of archeological information on the prehistory of Europe. Basically, she finds that his story of a highly developed civilization to the west that degenerated and changed from a source of peace and stability to an instigator of war makes sense of the archeological evidence, while the simplistic imagined history of humanity moving steadily up from a primitive state does not. (We are not yet able to correct by counting tree rings the carbon-14 dates further back than 4,500 B.C. But 4,500 B.C. in uncorrected dates corrects to 5,500 B.C., so it is altogether possible that the uncorrected date 8,500 matches 9,500 exactly.) Settegast's masterful book can be enthusiastically recommended to anyone trying to make sense of the prehistory of Europe, North Africa, and the Middle East.

Where was Atlantis? To me this question seems important if I am to use Steiner's work as a way to understanding the world as we encounter it, not as a teaching unrelated to what we can know with our senses. As you will see, I think there is a satisfactory answer, but if it is not satisfactory for you, please try to do better.

The current geological view—which would have been total heresy in Steiner's day—is that Europe, America, and Africa collided somewhere near the end of the Paleozoic, then recoiled and have been splitting apart steadily since then. There is no room in this view for an Atlantis which sank beneath the waves of the *mid* Atlantic somewhere around 10,000 B.C. The Mid-Atlantic Ridge, which in Steiner's time might have been thought to be sinking, is now seen as new material pushing up between the separating continents. But note that the priest speaks of the "Atlantic" as being not navigable in his own time because of mud where Atlantis had been. Now the Atlantic straight out from Gibraltar was certainly navigable, but the part of it that was of more interest, the European coastal waters, almost certainly had areas where mud was a problem, namely in the North Sea.

In 9,600 B.C., the sea level was 35 to 60 meters below its present level. (Different sources give different values.) There is a large shallow area in the North Sea extending from the present shore of the Netherlands out about 350 kilometers in a north-westerly direction to the outer edge of the Dogger Bank and running about 500 or 600 kilometers in length in a northeast to southwest direction. It all lies less than 35 meters deep now and would probably have been out of the water in 9,600 B.C. Deruelle has pointed out that this area matches Plato's description:

> The whole country was said by him [the priest] to be very lofty and precipitous on the side of the sea, but the country immediately about and surrounding the city was a level plain, itself surrounded by mountains which descended towards the sea; it was smooth and even, and of an oblong shape, extending in one direction three thousand stadia (about 560 km) but across the center of the island it was

two thousand stadia (about 370 km). This part of the
island looked towards the south and was sheltered from
the north. (*Critias*, 118, B. Jowett tr., Macmillan, London,
1892)

The size fits; the Dogger Bank would provide "the moun-
tains which descended towards the sea," quite precipitous on
the outer side, while the plain would have extended back in a
southwesterly direction towards what is now the Netherlands.
If we can accept "north" as meaning "northwest," the fit could
hardly be better. The "city" would have been on the southeast
side of the Dogger Bank, where there is still a strange circular
formation. The Dogger Bank, today rising only about 30
meters, undoubtedly got leveled off in the process of sinking
(Jean Deruelle, *De la préhistoire à l'Atlantide des mégalithes*,
Editions France-Empire, Paris, 1990).

When did it sink? The base of the Dogger Bank, where the
"city" should have been, presently lies at about -35 meters.
Establishing eustatic curves showing the sea level at earlier
times is tricky because the earth's surface has also been changing. According to the curve chosen by Deruelle (p. 206), it
would have gone under in about 7,500 B.C. Sources cited by
Settegast (p. 49) would seem to indicate a date close to 9,000
B.C., very close to the traditional date. Deruelle points to other
forces—uplift of the North Sea to offset the weight of the gla-
cier in northern Norway—which might have delayed the sinking; however, it seems to me that these forces may already be
in the eustatic curve he is using. It may also have been post-
poned by building dikes—but thereby made all the more quick
and dramatic when it came, set off perhaps by the invasion of a
victorious Athenian army or by "catastrophes of air and water."
Given the uncertainty in the process, it seems to me that there

is no problem in accepting the traditional date for the main disaster. The Dogger Bank itself and the more eastward part of the plain would have gone under later and might well have caused mud problems for coasting trade in the time of Solon, as well as being the source of the "sea peoples" who invaded the Mediterranean in the second millennium B.C.

(Deruelle somehow became convinced that to match Plato the end had to come in about 3,000 B.C. How he reached this conclusion has eluded me.)

The idea that Atlantis was to be found in the North Sea was originally put forward by Jürgen Spanüth in the early 1950's, and reworked by him in *Die Atlanter* (Grabert Verlag, Tübingen, 1976).

One may, of course, ask "If Atlantis was in the North Sea, why did Steiner say it was in the Atlantic?" Well, in the first place, the North Sea is part of the Atlantic, indeed one of the parts which mattered most to the ancients. I can also well imagine that Steiner's visions of the past did not always come with maps with precise, modern labels. Plato had put Atlantis in the Atlantic and there seemed little need to quibble. At times, Steiner placed it "west of Ireland" and there are banks extending several hundred miles west of Ireland which would have been out of water in 18,000 B.C. but would have gone under soon thereafter.

Paragraphs 91–99. Steiner's account of Atlantis is somber, one might even say frightening. It is a story of a struggle between "oracles" striving toward the spirit and fallen humanity sinking deeper into error under the influence of Luciferic and Ahrimanic beings. It is very different from the accounts of high-tech Atlantis one frequently finds. The chapters in *Cosmic Memory* on Atlantis provide many more details, including some seemingly magical high-tech.

ANCIENT PERSIA

It is not easy to find in the *Gathas* or hymns of Zarathustra a direct indication of the descent of Ahura Mazda into human incarnation. The closest that I have found is this:

Thus, with deep humility, we dedicate to Thee, O Ahura, and to Thy Law, as a votive offering, all the material creations in Thy Kingdom which fulfil themselves through the Good Mind, for upon the true visionaries descends from on high spiritual power as in one like You, O Mazda, for all time. (Yasna 34 v.3 in *Songs of Zarathushtra, The Gathas*, Dastur Framroze, Ardeshir Bode and Piloo Nanavutty, tr., George Allen and Unwin, London, no date)

EGYPT

105. The Greeks recognized their god Hermes (the Latin Mercury) in the Egyptian god Thoth. The role of this god in the foundation of Egyptian culture is central. He was the source of writing, the lord of knowledge, language, science and medicine; as moon god, he was lord of the stars and seasons; indeed it was he who called things into being by the sound of his voice. Thus, there is no problem at all in understanding Steiner's statement that the Mercury oracle was central to Egyptian culture. (See Garth Fowden, *The Egyptian Hermes*, Princeton University Press, Princeton, NJ, 1986, p. 22–23. This fascinating book is about the documents known as the Hermetic Corpus.)

It is also striking that Egyptian civilization took form very quickly, with the characteristic symbols appearing in the first dynasty. One who recognizes the existence of "oracles" and initiates sees here the effects of their work. Otherwise, one can only remark on the rapid transition. Steiner attributes this sudden burst of formative energy to the appearance in Egypt, presumably just at or before the beginning of the dynastic period, of a reincarnation of a disciple of Zarathustra but as an initiate of the Mercury oracle. He then says something like, "Borrowing a historical name, we may call him Hermes" (*Er sei in Anlehnung an einen geshichtlichen Namen "Hermes" genannt*). I do not read this sentence to mean that this initiate is a historical figure—one whom we can find in outer historical records. He certainly is not, and his name was almost certainly not Hermes, for Hermes is Greek, not Egyptian. Rather, Steiner needed a name for this figure for reference below and in his lectures. He chose a traditional one that pointed to his essence as an initiate of the Mercury oracle. Steiner mentions here that this "Hermes" was the reincarnation of a disciple of Zarathustra. In his lectures on the Matthew Gospel (GA 123, second lecture), he adds that this disciple received for this incarnation also the astral body of Zarathustra, while a second disciple received Zarathustra's etheric body for his incarnation as Moses.

Though "Hermes" is not a historical figure, there is a historical personality who may well be one of his successors. The first pyramid was built by the second king of the Third Dynasty, Djeser 2660–2680 B.C. With his reign is connected a remarkable figure, Imhotep (Imuthes in Greek), of whom Manetho is thought to be speaking when he says, "He was styled Asclepios in Egypt because of his medical skill. He was the inventor of building in hewn stone, and devoted attention to writing as well." This Imhotep "carried the titles of chancellor of Lower Egypt, royal prince, high priest of Heliopolis, chief of works, sculptor, carpenter, and so on" (Jean Vercoutter, *Egypte et la vallée du Nil*, Presses Universitaires de France, Paris, 1992, vol. 1, p. 250). His name is found, as sculptor, on a statue of the king. Here are all the traits of an initiate of the Mercury oracle, and it is not surprising that in the New Kingdom Imhotep was assimilated to the god Thoth, the Egyptian Hermes.

109. Steiner speaks of the two streams of initiation as the "mystical" and the "alchemical" in his article from 1917 "The Chemical Wedding of Christian Rosenkreutz" (GA 35, see especially pages 337–41. An English translation appears in Paul M. Allen, ed., *A Christian Rosenkreutz Anthology*, Rudolf Steiner Publications, Blauvelt, NY, 1968. See pages 23–25). What exactly is meant by developing soul capacities beyond the point necessary to perceive the sense world will become abundantly clear in the next chapter, for Steiner's own work is in this second stream, the one which is particularly counter to Ahriman. He says here specifically that this stream reveals the mystery secrets "over which Ahriman held his hand." The Adams translation renders the sentence literally. Attentive study of the context shows that those words can only mean that it revealed precisely what Ahriman wanted to conceal. Unfortunately, more than one reader may have come away with the impression clearly recorded in the Monges translation: "These mysteries were under Ahriman's influence." That is the opposite of what Steiner meant. These are the specifically anti-Ahriman mysteries. The Creeger translation, therefore, gives a correct interpretation rather than a literal rendering. The other mysteries are presumably anti-Lucifer, though that is less clear. These two streams are referred to repeatedly throughout the following paragraphs. In 110, Moses is said to be an initiate of both. In 112, the Christ works first to transform Lucifer and then Ahriman. In 114, the European mythologies are said to come primarily from the second type of mystery, although they contain elements of the first. Indeed the split in the soul seems to be simultaneous longings in the seemingly opposed directions of

these two streams. And in 115, the sixth age must bring them together. The second stream in more modern times is frequently called Rosicrucian by Steiner.

111. What Steiner says here of the Christ event is compressed to the extreme. He had far more to say about this event, which he regarded as the central, pivotal event of cosmic evolution. The best sources are his lectures on the gospels, which are probably best read in the order he gave them, namely, John (GA 103), Luke (GA 114), Matthew (GA 123), and Mark (GA 139). Other closely related lecture cycles are *The Apocalypse of St. John* (GA 104), *The Gospel of St. John in Relation to the Other Gospels* (GA 112), *From Jesus to Christ* (GA 131), and *The Fifth Gospel* (GA 148). The last concerns mainly the life of Jesus before the baptism and is based on Steiner's own reading of the akashic record.

In a chapter with so much about the hierarchies, it is natural to ask how the Christ being relates to them. The best explanation that I have found is this:

> That which was designated in the language of the Holy Rishis as Vishvakarma, in that of Zarathustra as Ahura Mazdao, in the Egyptian (if one really understands what stands behind the name) as Osiris and which we in the fourth period of civilization designate by the word "Christ" is that which has shone down through the portal of the Sun-spirit of Wisdom.... I do not say that the Sun-spirit of Wisdom alone shone through the Christ. He was the portal through which occult vision could be directed into infinite spheres, wherein are the spirits of the higher hierarchies; but the portal was the Spirit of Wisdom, the Sun-spirit of Wisdom. (*The Spiritual Beings in the Heavenly Bodies,* GA 136, lecture 9, April 1912)

Chapter 5

Knowledge of Higher Worlds: Initiation
Die Erkenntnis der höheren Welten

Themes

General Nature of Spiritual Training and the Need for It

1. Insight into higher worlds is achieved through the soul's remaining wide-awake and highly conscious while all sensory perception is excluded, as is normally the case only in sleep. This chapter will discuss methods to create such a state of consciousness. 2. The soul's awakening to this consciousness can be called initiation. 3. This awakening requires spiritual instruments of observation which are seminally present in everyone but need to be developed. While the development may happen spontaneously, training can enable us to meet our obligation to use fully all the capacities the wise guidance of spiritual beings has given us. 4–5. Appropriate instruction in no way permits others an undue influence in our lives, for we should understand how the rules and exercises work before using them. 6. Training may be particularly helpful to one who is close to self-initiation. 7. These practices have no direct influence on the part of our lives outside this domain, save that certain standards of moral conduct are necessary. No changes in the physical body's structure or operation are involved.

Exercises for Imaginative Cognition, Their Conditions and Consequences

8. The essence of the training is that the soul is to devote itself to specific mental images that have the intrinsic power to awaken hidden faculties. The best of these images are symbolic, but the essential point is that the soul devotes all its energies to the mental image with nothing else in its consciousness. 9–11. The rose-cross meditation (given here in full) illustrates this activity. 12. Many images could be used, but the object is always to tear the soul away from sensory perception and to rouse it to the development of inner faculties. One could, for example, meditate on *joy.* 13. Generally, meditation exercises must be carried out for a long time before the person doing them notices any result. 14. Not just any arbitrary thought content for meditation will lead to insights into higher worlds. 15. The path described here leads to *imaginative* cognition, so called because it is awakened by meditating on images. It stands next above the *object* cognition which is our normal waking consciousness. 16. Although similar to sleep in that the soul is released from the body, it is a state of heightened wakefulness. 17. The energy applied during meditation creates organs of soul and spirit; what is so created is also what is first perceived, so that our first perception is self-perception. The soul must have developed the will necessary to extinguish at any time all these images except that of the core of the soul's being which moves through repeated earth lives. 18. Having learned how to hold onto the mental images, the soul must then learn how to eliminate them yet remain conscious. In doing so, the soul frees itself from unconsciousness during sleep and develops a continuity of consciousness between sleeping and waking, at least for brief periods. Even this state is transitional to yet higher consciousness.

19. At this point, one becomes aware of a new being, a new I, aware of itself in a world of which one previously had no knowledge, and beside it, the old being, the old I. 20. The new I will begin to perceive spiritual realities and beings. This stage of development uncovers powerful egotism in us; training in will and moral development are necessary to be able to extinguish ourselves and overcome this egotism. 21. Previously acquired strength of logical thought and moral judgment must be shared between the new I and the old. It is therefore of utmost importance that they both be strongly developed before giving birth to the new I. 22. The exercises given here, therefore, emphasize developing our thought life.

23–29. Six soul qualities and exercises for developing them follow:

24. Objectivity and control of thoughts

25. Control of the will

26. Control of expressions of feelings

27. Positivity in thinking and feelings

28. Openness, unbiased receptivity to new experiences

29. Harmony among all of these.

30. These exercises help not only with the qualities specifically mentioned but also indirectly with others, such as self-confidence. It is valuable to set aside moments of inner tranquility and in them to fill our souls with communications from higher spiritual worlds. We will then find it possible to observe ourselves with the same objectivity with which we observe others. It is useful, in this respect, to review our day in reverse, looking at ourselves as if from the outside. 31. These prerequisites must be met, for our supersensible experience is built upon our foundation in ordinary life. Without a firm foundation, the supersensible experiences can develop improperly. Any immorality in our point of departure will cloud spiritual perception.

Sense-Free Thinking as a Spiritual Path

32. Letting such sense-free thoughts as exemplified in the previous chapters of this book "think themselves in us" supports the meditations. Human thinking can comprehend much more than we usually imagine it can. 33. Another, even more exact and perfectly safe path is found in the study of the author's philosophical works, which demonstrate that pure thinking, working only in itself, can unlock the secrets of the universe.

Organs of Perception

34. The goal of meditation on symbolic images is the creation in the astral body of active organs of perception. Metaphorically, these may be called "lotus flowers," but it is most important not to be misled by such names into sensory mental images of them. Indeed, the principal obstacle to perceiving in the spiritual world is preconceived ideas of how the perception is supposed to look. 35. Progress in these exercises requires so much patience that our best hope is to love them for their own sake, knowing that at the right time as much will come to us as is important for us to have. Indeed, absence of "flashes of light" may be a blessing, for partial success often delays complete success.

Levels of Consciousness: Imagination, Inspiration, Intuition

36. Four of the "lotus flowers" are named.

37–41. Above our ordinary "object" consciousness lie imaginative consciousness (37), inspirational consciousness (38–40), and intuitive consciousness (41). These words are used here in a special sense quite different from their usual meanings. In imaginative cognition, we recognize perceptions as emanations of soul-spirit beings which undergo constant transformation; inspirational cognition shows inner qualities of these beings and their relations to one another; with intuitive cognition we so penetrate other beings that we become, as it were, one with them. Reading the "hidden script" becomes possible. Recognition of the members of the human makeup and of the metamorphoses of *Saturn* into *Sun* into *Moon* into *Earth* are accessible to imaginative cognition. To follow the connection between *Saturn* and the present human physical body or the consequences of the separation of the sun from the earth, however, requires inspirational cognition. The recognition of the Spirits of Will, Wisdom, and others and their successive evolution requires intuitive cognition. Imagination can follow the human spirit in the states immediately following death up to purification in spirit land; inspiration can follow it further but there comes a point where even this "loses the thread." The essential innermost nature can then be followed only by intuition.

Exercises for Inspiration and Intuition and Their Effects

42–44. Exercises for inspirational cognition eliminate from consciousness the images of the sensory world used in exercises for imagination and concentrate on the spiritual activity which combined them. As with imagination, there are supporting exercises to strengthen the soul qualities necessary to do the main exercise. We should:

Retreat into ourselves at times to organize and digest our experiences, discovering new experiences in the old.
Openly receive impressions from the outer world and seek to understand them.
Seek to develop reverence and devotion to nature and to people.

Grow in self-awareness and self-confidence.

Note that at times something within us guides us better than the judgment we presently possess, yet not give in to "premonitions."

Ask not how to answer this or that question but how to develop faculties by patient inner work.

45. Many more qualities could be described, but in all cases steadiness and balance are the all-important soul qualities.

46. The exercises for intuition eliminate from consciousness also the student's own soul activity, which was the subject of attention in the exercise for inspiration. Nothing must remain of any previous inner or outer experience, yet something remains as an effect of these experiences. It is something really new, a perception through intuition.

Organs of Inspiration and Intuition

47. Just as the exercises for imagination developed the "lotus flowers" as organs of the astral body, so the exercises for inspiration and intuition develop currents and configurations in the etheric body. A new center for the etheric body forms in the head and then moves downward to the larynx and then to the area of the heart. Currents run from it to all parts of the body, especially the lotus flowers. A network of these currents surrounds the etheric body, making it self contained. At this point, it can come into contact with the external world of soul and spirit and inspirational consciousness begins. In it, percept and concept appear simultaneously, so that if we did not have this network we could not distinguish ourselves from our soul and spirit environment. 48. Similarly, the exercises for intuition reach also into the supersensible forces of the physical body.

Dealing with Illusion: the Lesser Guardian

49. On the path to higher cognition, thinking, feeling, and willing separate and become independent, but the separation should last only during supersensible observation. The I must then direct these three beings. 50–51. This experience is linked with another: Initially, the images of the world of soul and spirit change according to what we think or feel. We must therefore learn to distinguish ourselves from the rest of the spiritual world. To insure that we do so, our self-awareness in the world of the senses becomes a center around which gather all our likes and dislikes, passions, opinions, and so on. This "double" becomes the very first impression we meet when entering the spiritual world. As long as a hidden shame prevents us from facing it, it will also conceal the entire world of soul and spirit. Without all the preparation described previously, without recognition of the Luciferic influence in us, perceiving this being would destroy all our self-esteem, self-confidence, and self-awareness. The training and study described here are designed to give the strength to encounter the double. 52. Because this double makes itself invisible by the sense of shame and thereby conceals also the world of soul and spirit, it is also called the (lesser) guardian of the threshold. 53. If we entered the spiritual world without facing the guardian, we would fall into one deception after another, for we could not distinguish between this world and our own effects on it. 54. Besides confusing ourselves with the outer world, a further source of deception is misinterpreting the impressions we receive. If we form a wrong judgment of a supersensible process, that judgment will insert itself in the process and become so entangled with it that the two are not immediately separable. Truths and deceptions, however, can be recognized

by their makeup. The very nature of the exercises of inspiration and intuition holds the key. In the imagination exercises, there were elements taken from the sense world, so that our I did not really "get to the bottom" of the images. In the inspiration exercises, these images are removed and we look only at our own soul activity. But here too, error is possible, since our soul activity is influenced by upbringing, education, and so on, matters of which we cannot know the full origins. In the exercises of intuition, however, this activity is also removed. If anything remains, there is no aspect of it which cannot be known. Thus, intuition shows the makeup of something that is a total, clear reality in the world of soul and spirit. By applying the signs that can be recognized here as characteristic of reality to other experiences, reality can be told from semblance throughout the soul-spirit world.

Struggle with the Lesser Guardian,
Encounter with the Greater Guardian

55. The newborn I must struggle against the double, the old I, to insure that it does nothing contrary to the new I. When we compare the double to the newborn I, which also appears as an external soul phenomenon, the guardian changes form and appears as an image of the obstacles confronting the higher self in further development. If we shrink back, we become prisoners of the guardian, who again changes form, leading us to believe that we are at the pinnacle of knowledge. 56–57. In the original form of the guardian, we saw traits which were the result of Luciferic forces; in the new form, the guardian also shows what has happened to the soul under the influence of Ahriman. If we interpret the experience correctly, another figure soon appears, the greater guardian, who allows us to test ourselves for errors

of the second sort, misinterpretation (see paragraph 54). 58. The encounter with the (greater) guardian leads beyond personality to what is valid for every human being.

Microcosm and Macrocosm

59. As sketched in the previous chapter, every detail of the human makeup corresponds to a process or being in the outer world and its evolution. At the appropriate level, the student of the spirit recognizes these connections. The next step is then the feeling of becoming one with the macrocosm while being fully conscious of one's individual consciousness and independence. Seven steps of the initiation process are then enumerated: (1) study, (2) imagination, (3) inspiration, (4) intuition, (5) recognizing the relations of microcosm and macrocosm, (6) becoming one with the macrocosm, and (7) achieving a mood of soul that brings all these experiences together. 60. It is not necessary that one stage be completed before work can begin on higher ones.

The Greater Guardian as the Christ

61. The greater guardian becomes the example the student wants to follow. Once this happens, the greater guardian is transformed into the figure of the Christ. The student becomes a Christ initiate for whom the intervention and work of the exalted Sun-being, the Christ-being, in *Earth*'s evolution becomes direct experience.

62. The path described here can be followed by anyone today. It is different from the path that was followed in ages past, for the abilities and characteristics of souls change from incarnation to incarnation. Outer life has certainly changed since ancient times; and at any given time, outer life and initiation must be in perfect harmony.

Review Questions

What should a student insist upon knowing about a path of esoteric development before entering upon it?

What are the three levels of consciousness above our usual "object" consciousness? How would you characterize each? What is the nature of the exercises leading to each? In which bodies are the organs for each?

How is the rose cross symbol constructed and used meditatively? What is the purpose of using such symbols in meditation?

Why is it important to be able not only to hold on to mental images but also to extinguish them?

How is the egotism that arises in this work to be dealt with?

Why is it so important that logical thought and moral judgment be strongly developed before giving birth to the new I?

What are the six soul qualities or capacities which must be developed for imaginative cognition? What are the exercises for their development?

Why is the review of the day in reverse recommended?

What possible connection is there between Steiner's philosophical work—which makes no reference to higher worlds, beings or states of consciousness—and this chapter?

What is the "double" and how does it function as the guardian of the threshold?

What is the nature of the exercises for inspiration and intuition? What qualities need to be developed to support these exercises?

How does the nature of the exercises for inspiration and intuition enable the student to distinguish reality from illusion?

Describe the encounter with the greater guardian. What temptation arises here and how is it to be overcome?

Discussion Questions

Steiner mentions that the Matthew, Mark, and Luke gospels are written out of imaginative consciousness, while the John Gospel is written from intuitive cognition. In what ways do you notice this difference in reading them?

Does it seem strange—or does it make sense—that the newborn I must share with the old I the forces of logical thought and moral judgment developed in ordinary life?

The dangers of esoteric development seem immense and the path long, longer most probably than a lifetime. Does it really make sense to set out on this path? What is one to do during the possibly long period after some degree of imaginative consciousness has awakened and the time when intuitive cognition is reached and it becomes possible to distinguish reality from illusion in these matters?

During his lifetime, Steiner had a number of personal students of esoteric development, and this chapter reflects his work with them. In *How to Know Higher Worlds*, he stressed the value of a personal teacher. Few of his students have been willing to put themselves forward as advanced enough to help others. Meanwhile, however, there are innumerable others, not students of Steiner, who are ready and willing to teach esoteric development. What is the seeker to do?

Observations

A venerable tradition translates the word *Erkenntnis* in the title of this chapter as "knowledge." Yet the sense of *erkennen* is much more "to perceive, recognize." The Dutch have probably come close by translating the title of Steiner's *Wie erlangt man Erkenntnisse der höheren Welten?* as "How one gains *insights* into higher worlds."

Throughout this entire chapter, the reader should be aware that the original is written almost always in the *singular*—the student of the spirit, one, each, *Mensch*. Steiner could have used the plural had he wished. Presumably he used the singular to emphasize the fearsome aloneness which the seeker must feel. In the Creeger translation, the singular has almost always been changed to the plural to achieve "gender-inclusive" English, a requirement of the publisher. Consequently, at any moment, there are always two or more students on hand. The feeling of aloneness has been, unfortunately, lost.

8–30. There seem to be so many things to do that it may be useful to see how Steiner integrated them into a daily rhythm for individual students. A number of these have been gathered together in *Guidance in Esoteric Training* (GA 42/245). An example (see page 54) is shown as follows:

Evening:

Look back on the events of the day from evening till morning. Picture the blue orb of Heaven, with the great multitude of stars.

Devout and reverent	Fromm und ehrfürchtig
Let my soul send, expectant,	Sende ahnend
Its feeling sight	in Raumesweiten
into widths of space.	Meine Seele
	den fühlenden Blick.
May this sight receive	Aufnehme dieser Blick
And send	Und sende in
Into the depths of my heart	meines Herzens Tiefen
Light, Love, Life	Lichte, Liebe, Leben,
From spirit worlds.	Aus Geisteswelten.
(Soul peace)	(Sellenruhe)

Morning:

The mind pictures the Rose-Cross

What in this symbol	Was in diesem Sinnbild
The world's exalted Spirit	Zu mir spricht
Speaks to me,	Der Welten hohe Geist,
May it fill my soul	Erfülle meine Seele
At all times,	Zu aller Zeit
In all life's places,	In allen Lebenslagen
With Light, Love, Life.	Mit Lichte, Liebe, Leben.
(Soul peace)	(Seelenruhe)

Note that it involves the review of the day in reverse, picturing the blue night sky with many stars, and a mantra that sends the soul out, expectant, with feeling sight into the cosmos. One concludes in a moment of inner peace. Then, in the morning, it involves picturing the rose cross, meditating a mantra that focuses the spirit for all that may come during the day, and a moment of inner peace. An early meditation (from 1904, in GA 42 p. 146) begins with the ancient AUM. Note, at the beginning of the mantra given here its echo in the first word—*Fromm.* Such a combination as shown here was called a main exercise; and they varied, especially in the mantra, by student but always had the same elements. All students were given the six "side" exercises, which are here given in paragraphs 23–30. These "side" exercises (*Nebenübungen*) also appear in GA 42 under the title "General demands that anyone who wishes to undertake an occult development must impose on himself." They were mimeographed and given to all students. Because that version suggested adding one each month, they were also known as the "six-month" exercises. In *How to Know Higher Worlds* (GA 10), essentially the same six exercises appear as those for opening the twelve-petalled lotus flower mentioned here in paragraph 36.

34–36. As mentioned in the text, there is much more about the "lotus flowers" or chakras in *How to Know Higher Worlds*, especially in chapter 5, "Some Results of Initiation." Since half of the "petals" were previously developed and will open of themselves when the new ones are developed, each flower has half as many exercises as petals. The eight exercises of the sixteen-petalled lotus correspond to the eightfold path of Buddhism. The six exercises of the twelve-petalled flower are the six basic exercises of paragraphs 23–29. It may help to remember which flower is where to recall that we have sixteen teeth and twelve ribs on each side. The Sanskrit word *cakra* is related to the Greek *kyklos*, to the Old Slavonic *kolo*, and to the Anglo-Saxon *hweogul*, which was parent to modern English "wheel"— which is the root meaning of all of them.

47. The separation of percept and concept in ordinary, object consciousness is discussed in depth in Steiner's *Die Philosophie der Freiheit* (GA 4), variously translated as *The Philosophy of Spiritual Activity*, *The Philosophy of Freedom*, and *Intuitive Thinking as a Spiritual Path*.

54. In the expression that the guardian "poses a task" for the student, it seems clear that the word *poses* (*stellt*) is used as in "the leaking roof posed a task for John," not as in "the wise teacher posed a task for John."

Read literally, it appears from this section that the vision of being at the pinnacle of knowledge comes only to those who shrink from the vision of the work remaining to be done. The parallel with the temptations of Christ Jesus after the forty days in the wilderness (initiation), however, seems strong. He had not shrunk from the task that lay ahead, yet he beheld the vision of everything lying within his power if he would just yield. My impression is that the lesser guardian at this point alternates, at times showing how much remains to be done and at times appearing as the illusion of being at the pinnacle of knowledge. If we correctly interpret the vision and choose to go forward, we encounter the greater guardian. This encounter, described here with utmost brevity, is dramatically presented at the very end of *How to Know Higher Worlds*, GA 10.

59. On the subject of the correspondences between the microcosm and the macrocosm, see especially *Macrocosm and Microcosm* (GA 119) and *An Occult Physiology* (GA 128).

60. The observation that it is not necessary to complete one level of initiation before starting some work on the next may hold the key for understanding how the exercises of *How to Know Higher Worlds* fit with the structure of the present book. The earlier book laid out three stages—preparation, enlightenment, and initiation—and within each gave three (unnumbered) exercises. Thus, the preparation exercises involve (1) comparing growing and decaying, (2) listening to sounds, and (3) listening to speech. The enlightenment exercises are (1) comparing the stone and the animal, (2) meditation on a seed, and (3) contemplation of a person desiring something. Finally, initiation involves three trials, (1) fire, (2) water, and (3) air. There seems to me to be some connection between the first of each triplet of exercises and imagination, between the second of each triplet and inspiration, and between the third and intuition. I am not at all sure of this notion, however, and suggest it only to urge you to think about how the two books may fit together.

Chapter 6

Cosmic and Human Evolution:
Now and in the Future

*Gegenwart und Zukunft der Welt-und
Menschheitsentwickelung*

Themes

1. In the *Earth* stage of evolution, only part of the heritage of *Moon* condensed enough to be perceived by our senses. The supersensible world contains the other part, that which did not condense. As this other part is observed by supersensible consciousness, it seems to separate into two images. From the one can be pictured the ancient conditions. The other is now in a germinal condition, something that will take form in the future. The results of what happens on *Earth* flow into this future form which will represent the transformed *Earth;* we may call this the *Jupiter* planetary stage. Because of what happened on *Moon* and *Earth*, certain things will have to happen on *Jupiter*. Similarly, ancient *Sun* will be reflected in the *Venus* incarnation, and as a reflection of ancient *Saturn* will appear the future *Vulcan* incarnation. The mission of each of the present planets is described.

2. The spiritual researcher must be very careful in saying anything about the future, for statements about the future stir up feelings and will forces much more than do accounts of the past.

3–6. Just as in the planetary incarnations, so also in the smaller cycles, such as the cultural epochs, spiritual research can say something about the future. Our present age, the fifth, represents a reworking of the Egypto-Chaldean period but with the new forces born during the fourth age; the sixth will similarly rework the Persian age; and the seventh, the ancient Indian. The middle epoch, the Greco-Latin age, was thus a seminal moment. Three aspects of it are of key importance: (1) The capacity for intellectual reflection and logical thinking appeared and were strengthened by being cut off from direct interaction with the world of soul and spirit. (2) The type of modern spiritual training described in this book originated. (3) The Christ event occurred. Initially, this event could be comprehended out of the strength of spiritual traditions, but more and more, it became the task of the new initiates to grasp with their own faculties the content of the ancient mysteries and add an understanding of the Christ event. This task was made possible by the emergence through the new initiates of a hidden knowledge, a "science of the Grail." Thus, in the fifth period, the supersensible realities that had been perceived in dusklike consciousness in Egyptian times must again become known but imbued with personal forces of intellect, feeling, and comprehension of the Christ Mystery.

7. Following the seventh epoch will come an upheaval comparable in magnitude to the end of Atlantis or Lemuria and then a new "condition." But only souls who have succeeded in imbuing supersensible knowledge with their own forces of intellect and feeling at the transition from the fifth to the sixth post-Atlantean epoch will be mature enough to face the conditions which will then exist. Other souls will have to remain behind. In due course, the moon will reunite with the earth. Souls who have remained behind will temporarily form a distinct union of

evil in opposition to the good humanity. 8. The good portion of humanity will learn to use the moon forces to transform the evil part so that it can participate in further evolution as a distinct earthly kingdom. The earth then rejoins the sun and all together return to a spiritual state, from which will then emerge *Jupiter*. During the *Jupiter* condition, what are now minerals will have become plant-like; above the animal kingdom, which will have undergone a comparable transformation, will be the descendants of the "evil union," and above that the descendants of the community of good humans. Similar transformations occur on *Venus*, when a distinct cosmic body will break away containing all the beings who have resisted evolution and form an "unredeemable moon." Describing *Vulcan* is outside our scope.

9. The spiritualization that humans achieve in the fifth and sixth epochs through harmonizing the forces of intellect and feeling with knowledge of supersensible worlds will ultimately become the outer world. 10. Our future freedom depends not on predestined circumstances but on what our souls have made of themselves.

11. Just as we find ourselves in a cosmos of wisdom, so we also find ourselves as *independent* members of this cosmos because of the I received from the Spirits of Form. It is our work to develop from what we have received a *cosmos of love*. The manifestation of the exalted Sun being as the Christ is the encompassing example that leads the way. Wisdom is the prerequisite of love; spiritual knowledge plants the seeds which, reborn in the I, grow and ripen into love.

12. There is no fatalistic predestination in this description. No human soul is predestined to the "unredeemable moon." If all souls are too good for such bodies, the bodies will be ensouled by something other than former human souls.

Review Questions

How can future planetary incarnations be foreseen? What are their natures?

What are the origins and missions of the other present-day planets?

How are past epochs—Indian, Persian, Egypto-Chaldean—transformed in the future? What is the particular role of the Greco-Latin period?

How are past conditions—Atlantis, Lemuria—transformed?

What separations may have to occur among the present human souls? How will the progressive souls work with those that stay behind?

How and why can precisely we humans be the agents of creating a cosmos of love?

Discussion Questions

Does it make sense that in the Greco-Latin epoch the faculty for intellectual reflection and logical thinking was *strengthened* by being cut off from the soul and spiritual world?

In the transformation of past conditions—Atlantis, Lemuria—notice that there seems to be no transformation of the first two. In other words, the pivot is on the fifth condition rather than on the fourth, as in the epochs. Why do you think there is this difference?

Why could not higher beings just create a cosmos of love directly without taking the risky route of doing it through humans?

Is personal supersensible vision necessary for cooperation in the creation of the cosmos of love? How can one best cooperate in this work?

Observations

2. If you doubt that we are more sensitive to comments about the future than about the past, compare how you feel about the "Fall of anthropos" with your reaction to the "unredeemable moon" in paragraph 8.

3. "During the Egypto-Chaldean period, what we now know as logical thinking or grasping the world through reason did not yet exist." We can now read Egyptian stories, accounts of battles, and even hymns with reasonable accuracy and understanding. But when we come to sacred texts, we are lost. Before the hieroglyphs could be read, one could well imagine that the pyramids, tombs, coffins and papyri contained exalted philosophy. Instead, to modern minds, they make almost no sense at all. They seem to be notes on supersensible experience not at all penetrated by thought. In the Greco-Latin time "the capacity for intellectual reflection appeared." With Aristotle, we suddenly find a mind like our own looking at everything as if for the first time. He is asking What is logic? What are the laws of thought? What is the soul? What is substance? What do the parts of animals show us about how the universe hangs together? Aristotle wants to *think* about everything; he makes no appeal to any direct spiritual knowledge.

"The fourth period saw the first beginnings of the type of modern spiritual training that has been described in this book." This line is, I believe, another reference to the anti-Ahriman initiation mentioned in chapter 4, paragraph 109. What, precisely, is Steiner referring to? I do not think that he was referring to the mystery religions of the Mediterranean world. They seem to be the last echos of something ancient, not a new beginning. A more likely possibility might be Plato's Academy, which provided an education designed to equip students to understand the supersensible ideas. Mathematics, for example, played an important role, for it developed sense-free thinking. Aristotle went through this training and fully accepted its general thrust. He was as interested as Plato in concepts. In Neoplatonism and in the Hermetic Corpus, one finds many more examples of this thinking. Steiner's little meditation on joy in chapter 4 (paragraph 11) calls to mind the essays of Plotinus.

A whole different possibility is suggested by Steiner in a lecture entitled "The European Mysteries and their Initiates" (Berlin, May 6, 1909, printed in *Wo und wie findet man den Geist? GA 57*). In this lecture, from the same year in which he was writing this book, he traces a line of development from Celtic and Germanic mysteries through their becoming Christian and on into the Grail initiation and finally into the Rosicrucian stream, in which Steiner definitely felt himself to be working. It seems probable to me that he was referring to this stream, for it would explain the reference to the Grail in paragraph 5. I would certainly not discount, however, the importance of the first, the Greek stream, for the development of the tradition in which Steiner worked.

6. A few of the many ways in which Egypt reappears in our time can be mentioned. The sun god, Ra, was the center of Egyptian religion. We have put the sun in the center of the solar system. The Egyptians felt that humans were descended from the gods and depicted the gods as humans with animal heads. Many of our contemporaries have come to believe that humans are descended from animals. Our architecture has given up the arches of Roman and Gothic buildings for the post-and-lintel construction of the Egyptians. We have even taken to some degree of embalming of the dead.

The mention of the Grail calls to mind all the legends associated with it. The French and German sources on the Grail all received their present form in about a fifty-year period following 1175. The great English version, Thomas Malory's *Morte d'Arthur*, was written much later, in 1467. These stories show old Celtic supersensible knowledge in Christian transformation. There is much puzzling over exactly what the "Grail" was or is. In Wolfram's *Parzival*, it seems to be a stone. In other versions, it is the chalice of the Last Supper. From Steiner's description here it seems to me that it is really Christ-filled supersensible knowledge. Then the use of the term here makes excellent sense, as does the quest for it. The lecture on the European mysteries just mentioned is especially relevant here. Isabel Wyatt's *From Round Table to Grail Castle* (Lanthorn, East Grinstead, England, 1979) combines a good telling of the stories with interpretations based on the works of Steiner. John Matthews has gathered together many documents related to the Grail story in *Sources of the Grail* (Lindisfarne Press, Hudson, NY, 1996).

Also from Anthroposophic Press

How to Know Higher Worlds
A Modern Path of Initiation

RUDOLF STEINER
Translated by Christopher Bamford
Written 1904–1905 (CW 10)

This book begins with the premise that "the capacities by which we can understand the higher worlds lie dormant within each one of us." Steiner carefully and precisely leads the reader from the cultivation of the fundamental soul attitudes of reverence and inner tranquility to the development of inner life through the stages of preparation, illumination, and initiation. By patiently and persistently following his guidelines, new "organs" of soul and spirit begin to form, which reveal the contours of the higher worlds thus far concealed from us.

ISBN: 978 0 88010 372 5

Intuitive Thinking as a Spiritual Path
A Philosophy of Freedom

RUDOLF STEINER
Translated by Michael Lipson
Written 1894 (CW 4)

This seminal work asserts that free spiritual activity—the human ability to think and act independently of physical nature — is the appropriate path for people today who wish to gain true knowledge of themselves and the universe. This is not abstract philosophy; it is a warm, heart-oriented guide to the practice and experience of "living thinking." Readers will not find abstract philosophy here, but a step-by-step account of how a person may come to experience living, intuitive thinking—"the conscious experience of a purely spiritual content."

ISBN: 978 0 88010 385 5

Also from Anthroposophic Press

An Outline of Esoteric Science

RUDOLF STEINER

Translated by Catherine E. Creeger
Written 1910 (CW 13)

In this foundational work of spiritual science, we see how the creation and evolution of humanity is embedded in the heart of the vast, invisible web of interacting cosmic beings, through whom the alchemical processes of cosmic evolution continue to unfold. Included are descriptions of the various bodies of the human being, their relationship to sleep and death, and a detailed, practical guide to methods and exercises, including the "Rose Cross Meditation," through which we can attain initiation knowledge.

ISBN: 978 0 88010 409 8

Theosophy

An Introduction to the Spiritual Processes
in Human Life and in the Cosmos

RUDOLF STEINER
Translated by Catherine E. Creeger
Written 1904 (CW 9)

This key work is for anyone seeking a solid foundation in spiritual reality. Steiner presents a comprehensive understanding of human nature—from the physical body and the soul to our central spirit being. He provides, too, an extraordinary overview of the laws of reincarnation and karma and the various ways we live within the three worlds of body, soul, and spirit, describing the path of knowledge through which each of us can begin to understand the marvelously harmonious and complex worlds of soul and spirit.

ISBN: 978 0 88010 373 2